Benjamin Disraeli
Earl of Beaconsfield

Scenes from an Extraordinary Life

Benjamin
DISRAELI
Earl of Beaconsfield

Scenes from an Extraordinary Life

EDITED BY
Helen Langley

BODLEIAN LIBRARY
UNIVERSITY OF OXFORD

This catalogue is published to accompany the exhibition at the Bodleian Library
December 2003 – May 2004

© Essays: the contributors; catalogue: Bodleian Library, University of Oxford 2003

Published by
The Bodleian Library
Broad Street
Oxford OX1 3BG

ISBN 1-85124-094-2

Designed and typeset in Adobe Caslon by Dot Little at the Bodleian Library
Printed by University Press, Cambridge

Contents

FOREWORD

The groups of political papers at the Bodleian Library have grown to become one of the highpoint collections, attracting an increasingly international array of scholars, and underpinning significant research programmes within the University of Oxford. The deposit of the Disraeli Archive from Hughenden in the Bodleian in 1978 marked a significant addition to the collection, adding the papers of another Prime Minister to the Library's holdings (which now include the papers of six Prime Ministers). The Library's close cooperation with The National Trust has made the exhibition which coincides with this book possible, and we take great pleasure in thanking them for their assistance in all stages of planning, preparation and installation of the exhibition. Much of the success in developing these collections, in their promotion among scholarly communities, and in the curation of the exhibition and the creation of this book, is due to the efforts of Helen Langley, and it is with considerable pleasure that we record her major contribution to this project, and to the success of the wider political papers programme.

The exhibition curator, Helen Langley, was generously supported by a Millennium Award from Re:source, which funded a secondment to The National Trust. She was also assisted by Dr Timothy Mowl, Dr Roland Quinault, and Sir John Sykes, who commented on various sections of this book.

Staff in the Bodleian Library who have made possible this book and the exhibition include Tricia Buckingham, Nick Pollard and Nick Cistone from Imaging Services; Samuel Fanous, Gabrielle Brown and Dot Little from Communications & Publishing; Nicole Gilroy and Dana Josephson from Conservation; Colin Harris, Sam Hyde, Michael Hughes, Nigel James, Julie Anne Lambert, Gwydwr Leitch, Nick Millea, and Tim Rogers from Special Collections.

For location photography of items, very special thanks are due to Nick Pollard and Jane Inskipp, Nick Dunmur, and John Williams.

We would like to thank in particular the lenders to the exhibition, Annabel Jones, John and Virginia Murray, Professor Elizabeth Sykes, Sir John Sykes, and the several anonymous lenders.

Extracts from unpublished manuscript material appear by the permission of H. M. The Queen; Sir Isaiah Berlin's Literary Trustees, Collins Bartholomew, the Earl of Derby, The National Trust, the Hon. Mrs Crispin Gascoigne, Sir William Gladstone, Bt., the Earl of Iddesleigh, Henry Cobbold Lytton, John and Virginia Murray, the University of Reading, the Duke of Rutland, the Marquess of Salisbury and Sir John Sykes, Bt.

Extracts from editions of the *Benjamin Disraeli Letters* appear by permission of the University of Toronto Press. Attempts to locate the copyright owner of the Barbara Jones illustration taken from *Recording Britain* (1946) were unsuccessful.

The exhibition would not have been possible without the generous funding for essential conservation work on the archive, funded by the National Manuscripts Conservation Trust, The National Trust, and the Wolfson Foundation, 1978-98.

Reg Carr
Director of University Library Services and Bodley's Librarian

Disraeli, the Man and his Papers

Benjamin Disraeli, 1st Earl of Beaconsfield (1804–81) was an extraordinary man who led an extraordinary life. Disraeli is a very complex figure; a man of contradictions. To his contemporaries he was Sphinx-like, an attribute he shares with one of his successors, A. J. (later Earl) Balfour (1848–1930) – though Disraeli was less of a mystery to his immediate family. He has been described as an outsider who networked effectively in the establishment; a romantic with a willingness to engage in the realities of party politics; an opportunist but not without principles; and best-selling novelist with a substantial non-literary output. Socially mobile himself, he promoted 'One Nation' conservatism. He became proud of his Jewish antecedents and an upholder of the position of the Anglican Church. Disraeli had the ability to anticipate future trends. A traditionalist but not averse to risk, he took the view that 'change is constant'. He was driven by a Churchillian sense of destiny but lacked the Churchillian birthright to ease his path.

The proposal for the exhibition at the Bodleian Library originated in the late 1990s with Ros Lee at Hughenden Manor, Disraeli's former home and now a National Trust property. Disraeli's personal papers, the Hughenden Collection, catalogued in the 1960s by R. W. Stewart, have been held on deposit in the Library since 1978. The idea of creating a short biography based around the major stepping stones in Disraeli's life – or as many as could be documented by his papers and other collections in the Bodleian Library – was inspired by Nigel Nicolson's talk on his short biography of Fanny Burney during the 2002 Cheltenham Literary Festival.

The Hughenden papers are one of the Library's major nineteenth-century sources for the period. A large collection whose size was first decreased by assiduous weeding by Disraeli's lawyer, Sir Philip Rose, after Disraeli's death now runs to close on 1,100 boxes. In addition to Disraeli's political and literary papers it includes sizeable caches of those of his father Isaac, his sister Sarah, his wife Mary Anne Disraeli (created Baroness Beaconsfield in her own right in 1868) and of her first husband, Disraeli's Maidstone constituency colleague, Wyndham Lewis. Papers of Sir Philip Rose and Disraeli's official biographers, W. F. Monypenny and G. E. Buckle, form smaller sections. A very large proportion of the collection consists of incoming letters from many of the key figures of nineteenth-century Britain. The items selected for this publication show the pattern of Disraeli's relationships as much as the events under discussion.

The Library was extremely fortunate in being offered the loan of material from the John Murray Archive and from several private collectors including Annabel Jones, Sir John Sykes, Professor Elizabeth Sykes and Philip Waller. As a manuscript curator more familiar with the Library's twentieth-century collections than those from the nineteenth I am indebted to my fellow contributors to this publication who have drawn on their knowledge of Disraeli to write about different aspects of his life.

The Right Hon. Kenneth Clarke, QC, MP brings the insights of a former Chancellor of the Exchequer to his article on 'Disraeli as Chancellor'. Angus Hawkins, in 'Disraeli and the Earls of Derby', writes about Disraeli's relations with two of the key figures in his political career. Annabel Jones traces Disraeli's relationships with his publishers, focusing especially on Henry Colburn, and the House of Longman. Timothy Mowl explores the impact of Disraeli's novels on the writing of the elderly William Beckford. Roland Quinault evaluates the significance of Buckinghamshire for Disraeli, and Jane Ridley explores Disraeli's relationships with some of the key women in his life.

This publication is organized into ten chronological sections which are complemented by four additional sections, or galleries, consisting of images illustrating some of the key personalities, events and houses in Disraeli's life. The letters and artefacts selected here can provide only glimpses of a world which is both very distant and very near. What is striking is the smallness, by today's standards, of the political, literary and social circles in which Disraeli lived and worked, and the anti-Semitism which was often vicious and certainly commonplace in a manner which would not be tolerated today. Striking too are the several parallels between Disraeli and his twentieth-century successors (five of whose papers are held in the Bodleian Library) which, while not pointing to a prime-ministerial gene pool, raises questions about leadership traits and makes for some interesting comparisons.

Among the many items and images illustrated are the volume of correspondence with John Murray over *The Representative* newspaper (No. 12); the famous 'Mutilated Diary' (No. 31), first, and second editions of two of Disraeli's novels: *Vivian Grey* (No. 13) and *Sybil* (No. 50); a love letter from Lady Sykes (No. 33) and the previously unpublished painting of her by Daniel Maclise (No. 35); Mary Anne Disraeli's list of her own qualities and those of Disraeli (No. 44), letters from the 14th and 15th Earls of Derby (Nos. 68, 74, 93, 100, 118), the 3rd Marquess of Salisbury (Nos. 94, 95, 117), W. E. Gladstone (Nos. 71, 119), and Lydia Becker, a Women's Suffrage supporter (No. 97); a contemporary map illustrating the impact of the 1867 Reform Bill (No. 99), three letters from Queen Victoria (Nos. 106, 108, 110). Items normally on display at Hughenden include the small painting of Mary Anne Disraeli (No. 43), Disraeli's dispatch box (No. 123) and the Congress of Berlin fan (No. 121). Items on loan from private collectors include a selection of commemorative plates and jugs (Nos. 40, 76, 122, 132) and the publisher Thomas Norton Longman's memoir (No. 127).

The Disraeli exhibition has also been one of the projects selected by the recently-established Oxford Digital Library for digitization (with support from the Mellon Foundation). Work will begin on digitizing the exhibition as an educational resource after it closes in May 2004. The online version will be available in March 2005 from the Bodleian Library website.

Helen Langley
September 2003

Some Key Milestones in Disraeli's Life

1804–24		Born 21 December 1804
		Educated at Mr Potticary's School, Higham Hall near Walthamstow, and at home
	1817	Family converts to Christianity; Disraeli baptised
	1821	Articled to firm of solicitors
	1822	Changes spelling of his surname from D'Israeli to Disraeli
1824–31		Pupil barrister, Lincoln's Inn
	1824	Six-week tour, with his father and William Meredith, of Belgium and the Rhine
		In Germany decides to become a writer
	1824–5	Involves his father's friend, the publisher John Murray, in promoting speculative Mexican mining-company shares and takes leading role in the launch of Murray's newspaper, *The Representative*, with financially disastrous consequences
	1826	First novel, *Vivian Grey*, published
	1827	Nervous collapse brought on by debts, failures and frenetic lifestyle
	1829	The Disraeli family acquire permanent base in Buckinghamshire, Bradenham Manor
	1830	Has an affair with Clara Bolton, his doctor's wife
	1830–1	Health crumbles again. To recover and avoid creditors, travels with Meredith, his sister's fiancé, to Spain, Greece, Turkey, Cyprus, and the Middle East. Journey partly financed by income from his 1831 novel, *The Young Duke*
1832–7	1832	*Contarini Fleming* published
		Unsuccessfully contests High Wycombe as Independent Radical
	1833	Unsuccessfully stands as Independent Radical in Marylebone election
	1833–6	Affair with Lady Sykes
	1835	After failing three times to be elected as a Radical unsuccessfully contests Wycombe as a Conservative
	1835	*Vindication of the English Constitution* published
	1836	*Henrietta Temple (A love story)*, a fictionalized account of the affair with Lady Sykes, published December 1836 (dated 1837)
	1837	Wyndham Lewis returned as one of two Conservative MPs for Maidstone in Kent
		Makes disastrous maiden speech
	1839	Marries Mary Anne Wyndham, widow of Wyndham Lewis
	1841	Conservative MP for Shrewsbury
1842–5		Leading figure in Young England faction of the Conservative Party
		Declares himself a supporter of the Corn Laws on political, economic and social grounds
	1843	Attacks Peel's leadership, especially over his plans to repeal Corn Laws; loses party whip
	1844	*Coningsby* published, the first political novel and first volume in the trilogy *Coningsby*, *Sybil*, and *Tancred* in which Disraeli explores his ideas on contemporary social conditions, political and constitutional issues, and religion
	1845	*Sybil* published; second volume of the trilogy

1845–59	1845–9	Major figure in Protectionist faction of Conservative Party
	1846	Spearheads destruction of Peel's leadership
	1847	*Tancred*, the final novel in the trilogy, published
	1847–76	MP for Buckinghamshire
	1848	Purchases Hughenden Manor
	1849	Effectively Leader of the Protectionists in the House of Commons, but position not secure
	1851	Biography of the late Lord George Bentinck, the former leader of the Protectionists, published
	1852	February: Chancellor of the Exchequer in Lord Derby's short-lived minority government. His budget marks his return to party's mainstream
	1853	Establishes and is a leading contributor to the weekly newspaper *The Press*, a vehicle for progressive conservatism, which was also targeted at disaffected moderate Whigs
1859–67	1858–9	Chancellor of the Exchequer and Leader of the House of Commons in Derby's minority Government. His (1859) Reform Bill defeated by Liberals
	1866–7	Following defeat of Liberals Reform Bill returns to Government as Chancellor for third time. Successfully introduced Second Reform Bill
1868–72	1868	On Lord Derby's retirement from politics, becomes Prime Minister of the Conservative minority Government; resigns after December election
	1872	Crystal Palace Speech defining tenets of Disraelian conservatism
		Death of Mary Anne Disraeli
1874–80		Heads first Conservative majority Government for nearly thirty years. The Government introduces the largest tranche of social legislation by a nineteenth-century administration including the Trades Union, Public Health Artisan Dwellings and Factory Acts
	1875	Purchases shares in the Suez Canal
	1876	Declares Queen Victoria Empress of India
		The Eastern crisis erupts. Disraeli's response to news of the Bulgarian Atrocities sharply criticized. Cabinet divided over policy towards Russia and Turkey
		In poor health and stressed, he leaves the House of Commons; as Earl of Beaconsfield he leads the Government from the House of Lords
	1878	With Lord Salisbury, the Foreign Secretary, attends Congress of Berlin to settle the 'Eastern Question'
		Clashes with Gladstone again over Government's handling of the Eastern Question and the acquisition of Cyprus
	1880	Retires after Conservatives defeated at the polls
		Final novel *Endymion* published
	1881	19 April: dies at his London home, 19 Curzon Street. Leaves instructions that he is not to be given state funeral. Honouring a promise made to Mary Anne, he is buried alongside her at Hughenden Church.

Fig. 1 **Cartoon,** *Vanity Fair* (Jan. 30, 1869, No. 13, Statesmen, No. 1), 29 x 19 cm; reproduced by permission of a private collector. The caption poses the question whether becoming what he is from what he was is Disraeli's greatest reform of all.

Disraeli as Chancellor

I FEAR THAT my great political hero, Benjamin Disraeli, was a disastrously bad Chancellor of the Exchequer. I admire Disraeli as a politician for his subtle intellect, his tactical genius, his sense of the national interest and his strong social conscience. However he should never have been appointed Chancellor of the Exchequer and he had the misfortune to hold the office three times.

His first experience was the worst. In 1852 the Chancellorship was the first political office he had ever held. He produced a Budget which was so politically disastrous that the short-lived government led by Lord Derby lost office upon its rejection.

Upon first taking office, Lord Derby had felt obliged to make Disraeli Leader of the House of Commons, which made him the Conservative Government's chief spokesman in the House of Commons. The only reason that Derby also made him Chancellor of the Exchequer was because the Prime Minister was quite determined to refuse to appoint him Foreign Secretary as Disraeli would have preferred.

Disraeli had no understanding of money nor experience of political economics. As a result of reckless youthful speculation he was quite hopelessly in debt personally. He was so insolvent that if he had been defeated in an election and lost his parliamentary immunity he would soon have found his way to a debtor's prison. The then substantial salary of the Chancellor was very welcome to him.

On budgets and financial policy Disraeli said when in office 'My own knowledge on the subject is of course recent. I was not born and bred a Chancellor of the Exchequer. I am one of the Parliamentary rabble.' Expressing doubts on his own appointment, he was famously told 'they give you the figures'. Unfortunately for him this confident forecast proved wrong. The Treasury let him down by failing to explain to him the complexities of the tax system and by giving him forecasts of the public finances which eventually proved to be wrong.

He was a member of the weak minority Government formed by the Protectionist recently pro-Corn Law wing of the Conservative Party, split from its Peelite wing. The Cabinet was packed with obscure aristocratic grandees and it was known as the 'Who? Who?' Government because of the reaction of the then deaf Duke of Wellington as the names of its Ministers were read out to him. Disraeli was secretly hoping to persuade the Party to abandon protectionism and return to free trade and unity with the Peelites. However he felt obliged to tailor a Budget to pander to his protectionist back-benchers and the landed interest.

The Peelites would only abstain from direct opposition and allow Derby to hold office on condition that an early General Election would be held. This meant that the Budget had to be presented early in November 1852. I am the only Chancellor of modern times to have delivered all my budgets in the month of November. In 1852 this was too early in the financial year to make an accurate forecast of the public finances. The Treasury were extremely pessimistic and Disraeli was only able to produce the then obligatory balanced budget by making use of a very dubious technicality.

There was no welfare state in 1852 and few public services. Public expenditure was dominated by military and particularly by naval spending. After the government took office the country was gripped by an unfounded scare about a war with France. Derby made Disraeli's problems worse by insisting on raising the estimates for the Royal Navy by the enormous sum of £1 million, in order to strengthen protection against the supposed threat of an invasion by Louis Napoleon.

This appalling combination of circumstances faced by this weak Government and this ill-prepared Chancellor help to explain, although they do not excuse, the dog's breakfast of a Budget which Disraeli produced.

The popular 'sweetener' in the Budget was supposed to be a reduction in the Malt Tax. This pleased the protectionist agricultural interest and compensated them for the Government's inability to reintroduce the Corn Laws. It also had the happy consequence of reducing the price of beer. Disraeli tried to cheer up urban middle-class households by a remission of the duties on tea. For remission, he turned to the House Tax and to Income Tax. The increase in the House Tax hit the householders who dominated the then electoral franchise.

Income Tax was then regarded as a temporary expedient and Disraeli's distinguished predecessor, Sir Charles Wood, had only managed to persuade Parliament to extend it for one year at the rate of 7p in the pound. Disraeli made an early effort at stealth taxes by a complicated restructuring which attempted to set different rates for so-called earned and unearned income. The tax was based on a mass of complicated schedules which the Treasury failed to explain properly and which Disraeli failed to understand. All his proposals had unintended consequences and produced unfair anomalies. One change was clear in its effect. He lowered the threshold for the tax from earnings of £150 a year to £100 and made large numbers of lower earners liable to pay the income tax for the first time.

Disraeli produced this to a House of Commons in which the Opposition could field three distinguished ex-Chancellors who between them had produced the previous thirteen Budgets. He was also faced by Cobden and Bright and the powerful Manchester group of free traders. They helped the House to understand that Disraeli's Budget hit the urban middle classes very hard in order to benefit the landed interest and the aristocracy.

Disraeli's attempts to win the vote on his unhappy proposals were heroic but futile. On the final evening he spoke for five hours in what was expected to be the concluding speech of the debate. Some thought he had perhaps drunk a little too much beforehand. He was clearer in his attacks on his political enemies than he was in his explanation of his financial measures. But he must have sat down relieved if exhausted.

Unexpectedly, in a House about to have a division, the young rising star of the Peelite Party rose to reply to the Chancellor. Speaking for a mere three hours, William Gladstone proceeded to display his own mastery of the subject of the public finances and to destroy every feeble argument in favour of the Budget. The Government lost the subsequent vote and fell from office.

The ultimate irony was that William Gladstone was, not surprisingly, appointed as Disraeli's successor at the Treasury. He succeeded to a golden inheritance. There was no war, the estimates had been wrong and he had a large budget surplus. Gladstone was enabled to produce the greatest Budget of his career, establish the office of Chancellor of the Exchequer in its modern form and make the reputation which eventually took him to the Premiership.

For Disraeli, his only consolation was the Chancellor's set of robes which he kept as a souvenir and refused to hand on to Gladstone, who was obliged to buy his own.

How can a modern admirer of Disraeli like me, who also happens to have been Chancellor of the Exchequer, explain this absurd episode in the career of the man who was one of the chief architects of the modern Conservative Party and became the idol of its liberal 'One Nation Tory' wing? Firstly and obviously, his eventual achievements were in other fields than economic policy – imperial policy and foreign policy leading up to the Congress of Berlin; conservative social policy combined with enlightened reforms to improve the condition of the industrial working class and so on. But even in the travails of 1852, Disraeli appears to have enhanced his reputation for dominance in Parliamentary debate and political management. He was almost single-handed as spokesman in the Commons for the Derby Government on every important subject and not just the Treasury. The Conservative Party must have begun to realise, however appalling the thought was to some of them, that they would have no alternative eventually but to turn after Derby to this unlikely figure as his successor as party leader. On the occasion of the Budget debate, Gladstone may have had the best arguments to hand. But the clash between Disraeli and Gladstone was the most dramatic evidence thus far of the forthcoming dominance by these two men of later Victorian politics. On ground better suited to his talents, Disraeli would have his revenge on later occasions.

Kenneth Clarke

Disraeli and the Earls of Derby

AFTER 1846 Benjamin Disraeli's remarkable political career became closely woven around the influence of the Derby dynasty. The earls of Derby were the pre-eminent aristocratic family of mid-Victorian Conservatism. Disraeli's relations with the 14th and 15th Earls of Derby, (see Nos. 56, 78) initiated amid scandal, moving towards hard-won respect and concluded with disaffection, traced the trajectory of his career. To Edward Geoffrey Stanley, 14th Earl of Derby (1799–1869), he was, as his Commons leader from 1849 to 1868, a long-serving lieutenant. Disraeli was Chancellor of the Exchequer in all three of Derby's Conservative governments in 1852, 1858–9 and 1866–8. To the younger Edward Henry Stanley, 15th Earl of Derby (1826–1893), Disraeli was an early mentor, beguiling confidant and, by the late 1870s, an estranged party leader.

Disraeli's first direct contact with the Stanley family was shrouded in scandal. On board the ship returning him from his tour of the Middle East, in the autumn of 1831, Disraeli befriended the future 14th Earl of Derby's wayward younger brother, Henry Stanley. After landing at Falmouth the two men travelled to London together. Then, to the alarm of his family, Henry Stanley disappeared, eventually to be discovered in the notorious gambling house known as 'the Hell' on St. James's Street. Perhaps unfairly, Henry's family blamed the immoral influence of Disraeli for this embarrassing episode. Certainly it created in the mind of Henry Stanley's elder brother a strong prejudice. The hostility of the Stanley family was promptly added to the numerous obstacles blocking Disraeli's path to political preferment. In 1841 the future 14th Earl, styled Lord Stanley from 1834 to 1851, was appointed Colonial Secretary in Sir Robert Peel's Conservative ministry. He fiercely objected to the dandy, novelist and debtor Disraeli being given a junior office. Reportedly he declared to Peel that 'if that scoundrel' was in the ministry he would not remain himself.[1]

Then, in 1846, both Disraeli and Lord Stanley unexpectedly found themselves aligned in opposition to Peel's Repeal of the Corn Laws. In the Commons the forty-two year old Disraeli became the acerbic mouthpiece of backbench indignation at the apostasy of their Peelite leadership. In the Lords the forty-seven year old Stanley reluctantly accepted the leadership of the Protectionist Conservatives. As the rising hope of the moderate Whigs in the 1820s, Stanley had embraced George Canning's liberal Tory agenda of Catholic Emancipation, government economy and moderate parliamentary Reform. As Lord Grey's Chief Secretary for Ireland after 1830 he was thrust into the cauldron of Irish politics; combating Daniel O'Connell in the Commons, enforcing the rule of law in an Ireland disrupted by rural violence, and playing a crucial role in the success of the 1832 English Reform Act. On taking up the Colonial

Secretaryship in 1833 he oversaw the abolition of slavery in the British Empire. Then, in 1834, he broke from his more advanced Whig colleagues and, after forming a short-lived centrist party dubbed the 'Derby Dilly', began to move over to the Conservative Party. By 1838 Stanley's early Whiggism had become assimilated within Peelite Conservatism. As part of his Whig apprenticeship, however, Stanley had been taught the central importance to the preservation of liberty and progress of cohesive parliamentary parties. Only by good men combining at Westminster could a capricious prerogative and an unruly populace be restrained. But in 1846, by dramatically converting to Free Trade, Peel violated the necessary mutual trust between political leaders and their backbench support.

'Civil war', Sir Walter Scott wrote, 'is a species of misery which introduces men to strange bedfellows.' Certainly the Conservative schism over Corn Law repeal brought Stanley and Disraeli together as unlikely political associates. The two men were strikingly dissimilar, sharply divided by background, upbringing, temperament, education and social station. Educated at Eton and Christ Church, Oxford, Stanley was heir to the second oldest earldom in the kingdom and widely recognised for his cleverness and oratorical ability. He was self-assured and patrician in manner. As a young man he was called 'the hope of the nation' by William Huskisson. He assumed a leading role in national affairs almost by birthright. Alongside politics he was devoted to the aristocratic pleasures of field and turf, while also spending time in his library translating Homer. An insouciant social manner cloaked his political seriousness. He portrayed public duty as an obligation of his birth and affected a lofty indifference to personal distinction. But those who dismissed him as a dilettante confused manner with motivation. An earnest commitment to the nation's interests lay behind the public appearance of effortless unconcern.

By contrast the largely self-taught middle class Disraeli patently looked to become a hero in the world. The realisation of his genius through individual struggle gave impetus to his sense of personal destiny. Byronic Romanticism had shaped his youthful sensibilities. As he wrote in his 1832 novel, *Contarini Fleming*, he entertained 'a deep conviction that life must be intolerable unless I were the greatest of men'. Disraeli had no taste for rural pursuits and never learnt to ride a horse. While visiting Yorkshire in 1853 he complained that 'living much in the air' had 'demoralised my intellectual capabilities'.[2] For Disraeli, public distinction was the valued prize to which he devoted his heroic struggle against prejudice and social bigotry.

Disraeli's ironic postures and patent ambition grated on Stanley's patrician sensibilities. It was only in 1849 that Disraeli was appointed by Stanley to the Conservative leadership in the Commons, other more orthodox Conservative MPs having been tried and found wanting. None possessed Disraeli's ability to humiliate their opponents by the force of their razor-edged rhetoric. But, as Disraeli recognised, Stanley saw him as a man to be used, but not to be relied upon. Stanley acknowledged Disraeli's talent, but mistrusted his intentions. In turn, while solicitously deferential in his exchanges with Stanley, Disraeli was often privately scathing about his leader's shortcomings. In his eulogistic biography of Lord George Bentinck, written during the recess of 1850, Disraeli portrayed Stanley as a secondary personage in the party. Theirs was a relationship born of public necessity rather than personal warmth. Stanley, who succeeded his father as 14th Earl of Derby in 1851, never visited Disraeli at Hughenden. Not until December 1853 was Disraeli invited to the Derby's family seat at Knowsley. The visit, moreover, was not a success. Derby affected to be much bored by Disraeli's arrival, while Disraeli was sharply critical of Knowsley and the social failings of his hostess. Derby's patrician aloofness was guaranteed to inflame the defensive barbs of Disraeli's insecurity. The social chasm between the two men never seemed greater than when they came together under the same roof at Knowsley.

Their relationship was founded on Derby's need for Disraeli's abilities and the necessity to Disraeli of Derby's endorsement. While the Conservatives were in opposition, which they were for most of the 1850s and 1860s, the strains in their relationship were at their most acute. Disraeli's tactical ingenuity constantly unsettled Derby. During 1849 Disraeli sought to wean the Conservatives from Protectionism, formulating an alternative fiscal policy equalising and extending direct taxation. A provoked Derby reprimanded Disraeli for 'a somewhat hasty promulgation of crude and lightly-considered schemes'.[3] Likewise, in 1853 Derby's suspicions of Disraeli were exacerbated by Disraeli's pursuit of implausible alliances with the Irish Brigade, discontented Whigs, and English Radicals such as Thomas Milner Gibson, John Bright and Richard Cobden. When Disraeli launched his journalistic mouthpiece, *The Press,* in 1853 Derby strongly disapproved. Disraeli's attempt, during the same period, to fashion himself into an unlikely champion of militant Anglican Protestantism drew fierce rebukes from Derby. In October 1855, while British troops were fighting in the Crimea, Derby was outraged by Disraeli's advocacy of a peace opposition policy in alliance with the radicals and the Peelites. Only with great difficulty did Derby keep Disraeli 'riding to orders'. [4] Opposition to a resourceful Lord Palmerston, as premier after 1855, brought Derby's relations with Disraeli to a chilling low. As a result, in 1856, Disraeli sullenly withdrew from the political fray, refraining 'from saying, doing or writing anything which should bring my views, or even name, before the country'. [5]

For his part Disraeli was frustrated by Derby's advocacy of 'masterly inactivity' in opposition and was infuriated by Derby's refusal to accept office in February 1851 and February 1855. The first occasion a mortified Disraeli described as a 'ludicrous catastrophe'.[6] The second occasion, he complained, threatened the Conservative Party with ruin. But, for good reason, Derby refused to accept power on sufferance under terms dictated by his opponents. It was 'a bungling fisherman', he observed, 'who strikes at the first nibble'.[7] With patrician calm Derby looked to play the longer game, while the restless and ambitious Disraeli chafed at what he saw as great opportunities cast casually aside.

In public, however, Derby was always careful to endorse Disraeli's authority. In a Commons party shorn by the crisis of 1846 of talent and experience, he recognised that Disraeli was the most effective orator the Party Possessed. As he shrewdly observed to Queen Victoria in 1851, who was alarmed by the mercurial Disraeli, 'men who have to make their own positions will say and do things which are not necessary to be said or done by those for whom positions are provided.'[8] To the Party he repeatedly defended Disraeli as a man of high ability, vivid imagination and great eloquence. Despite his private reservations about Disraeli's trustworthiness, Derby recognised the need Conservatives had of Disraeli's talents. In opposition to Palmerston's second Government from 1859 to 1866 Disraeli showed a greater willingness to accept Derby's strategy of 'killing with kindness' – opposition quiescence allowing ministerial differences to come to the fore, although, as a consequence, Disraeli was often during 1863 and 1864 absent from the Commons and a peripheral figure in parliamentary debate.

When working together in government Disraeli's relations with Derby were more harmonious. In office Disraeli shed the provocative postures of his youthful dandyism and assumed the air of a statesman. Derby was the first British politician to become Prime Minister three times, in 1852, 1858–9 and 1866–8. In each of Derby's governments Disraeli served as Chancellor of the Exchequer and leader of the Commons. As Chancellor in 1852 Disraeli, with Derby's support, abandoned Protectionism in a speech the Prime Minister judged 'a masterly performance.' In 1858 Disraeli stepped forward as a prudent and resourceful Chancellor demonstrating that the Conservatives were capable of responsible government. Likewise, from 1866 to 1868 he oversaw the nation's finances in a manner that corroborated Derby's broader claim that the Conservatives could deliver stable government safeguarding moderate progress. It was in 1867, however, that Disraeli finally came into his own as the Government's leading spokesman. The sixty-eight year old Derby was chronically ill and his grasp on events weakening. Yet Derby had already committed his Government to a substantial measure of parliamentary reform. This was a replay of 1858–9 when, despite Disraeli's reluctance, Derby had pledged his ministry to a Conservative Reform bill. Honouring an irrevocable undertaking in 1867, Disraeli, notwithstanding his earlier hesitation, seized on extensive reform as a means of scattering a powerful Liberal opposition. The resulting 1867 Reform Act enfranchised one in every three adult males in England and Wales. As Derby saw and Disraeli belatedly recognised, this shattered the Liberal pretence to be the monopolists of progressive legislation.

In October 1869 the 14th Earl of Derby died and an unlikely association, based on mutual need and grudging respect, came to an end. Derby's eldest son Edward Henry Stanley succeeded to the title. As a young man fresh up from Cambridge, the 15th Earl, styled Lord Stanley from 1851 to 1869, had been much enamoured of Disraeli's lively conversation and political imagination. After 1849 he became a frequent visitor to Hughenden. He marvelled at Disraeli's 'singleness of purpose – contempt of obloquy – energy which no labour can exhaust – indifference to the ordinary pleasures and pursuits of man, which he neglects in search of power and fame'. [9] In Disraeli's company he found an exhilarating exoticism that enlivened the more orthodox patrician perspectives of Knowsley. When he read Disraeli's novel *Lothair* in 1870 he recognised in the work an 'almost childish love of what is gorgeous and striking; the same oriental turn of mind that induces my friend like most of his race, to take pleasure in striking exhibitions of colour'.[10] For many Conservatives the future 15th Earl was, during the 1850s, 'the coming man' and a future replacement for Disraeli as Commons leader. But such hopes were frustrated by Stanley's dislike of Tory obduracy, his concern for his own political independence, and his temperamental distaste for the compromises necessary to effective leadership. The conscientious and industrious Stanley became, arguably, the best party leader the Victorian Conservatives never had. Moreover, by 1855 he was spending increasing time in the congenial company of the political hostess Lady Salisbury at Hatfield House. To Derby's relief his eldest son gradually moved away from Disraeli's orbit. Stanley's intelligence and administrative ability, however, were affirmed by his achievements as Colonial Secretary and Foreign Secretary in his father's cabinets in 1858–9 and 1866–8.

In 1870 the 15th Earl of Derby enabled Disraeli to continue as Conservative leader by declining the position for himself. He wished to be 'a neutral, singularly free from pledges or ties'.[11] Thus, at a decisive moment, the next generation of Stanleys helped to preserve Disraeli's precarious authority. In 1874, when the aged and ill Disraeli finally became prime minister, the younger Derby agreed to serve as his Foreign Secretary. But all youthful enchantment had now gone. Derby regarded the elderly Disraeli's fawning on the reclusive Queen Victoria as distasteful vulgarity. The severing of political ties between the two men finally came in 1878 due to what Derby saw as Disraeli's swaggering bellicose posturing; Derby abhorring the Prime Minister's careless talk of war with Russia during the Bulgarian Crisis. On 27 March 1878 Derby resigned from Disraeli's cabinet, believing his old friend to have privately conspired against him. Thirty years of party leadership, Derby concluded, had encouraged Disraeli narrowly to regard all great national questions from an almost exclusively parliamentary point of view. When Derby unexpectedly encountered Disraeli in a London street in March 1879 he noted in his journal that he had 'no wish to see the old man again, or to renew personal intercourse'.[12] By Disraeli's death in 1881 Derby was well along the path to Gladstonian Liberalism. In a melancholy recollection of their earlier close friendship, Derby recorded that Disraeli's 'part was played, his name is inscribed in the history of England, he had held supreme power, and for some years had enjoyed a vast reputation'. But it was a blessing that he 'died while his mind was still clear, and while his fame was fresh. Neither might have been the case five or six years hence, and no man would have felt more painfully the appearance of neglect'.[13]

Angus Hawkins

1   W. F. Monypenny and G. E. Buckle, *The Life of Benjamin Disraeli, Earl of Beaconsfield*, 6 vols. (London, 1910-1920), II. 122.
2   M. G. Wiebe, Mary S. Millar, Ann P. Robson (eds.), *Benjamin Disraeli Letters Volume VI: 1852–1856* (Toronto, 1997), p. 208: Disraeli to Edward Henry Stanley, 26 January 1853.
3   Monypenny and Buckle, *Disraeli*, Stanley to Disraeli, 22 September 1849, III. 215.
4   Malmesbury to Derby, 8 September (1853) Derby Mss 144/1 Liverpool Record Office.
5   Disraeli to Derby, 7 November 1855 Derby Mss 145/3 Liverpool Record Office.
6   H. M. Swartz and M. Swartz (eds.), *Disraeli's Reminiscences* (London, 1975), p. 49.
7   J. Vincent (ed.), *Disraeli, Derby and the Conservative Party, the Political Journals of Lord Stanley, 1849-1869* (Hassocks, 1978), p. 44.
8   Swartz and Swartz (eds.), *Disraeli's Reminiscences*, p. 43.
9   Vincent, *Disraeli, Derby*, p. 33.
10 J. Vincent (ed.), *A Selection from the Diaries of Edward Henry Stanley, 15th Earl of Derby (1826-93) between September 1869 and March 1878*, Camden Fifth Series, Vol. 4 (London, 1994), 61.
11 Ibid., p. 45.
12 J. Vincent (ed.), *The Diaries of the 15th Earl of Derby between 1878 and 1893: A Selection* (Oxford, 2003), p. 105.
13 Ibid., p. 320.

Fame and Reputation: A Novelist and his Publishers

DISRAELI'S RELATIONSHIPS with his publishers span not only the larger part of the century (his first published novel *Vivian Grey* appeared in 1826, and his last *Endymion* in 1880) but involved two publishers in particular, each of a very different nature. Disraeli was loyal to Henry Colburn, but it was not until he began to publish with the House of Longman in 1864 that he had a relationship with a publisher that grew beyond the bounds of mere business. His father enjoyed a similarly long and close relationship with John Murray II (1778–1843), but Disraeli jettisoned that (and his father's) in the affair over *The Representative*, although Murray did (briefly) become his publisher for *Contarini Fleming* and *Gallomania* in 1832.

Colburn's date of birth is uncertain though he died in 1855. In 1816 he was already the owner of Morgan's Circulating Library in Conduit Street. Michael Sadleir notes that he was publishing in 1807, and by 1814 his list already ran to nine pages at the end of Lady Morgan's novel, *O'Donnell*.[1] Colburn has been described as 'the Rupert of Hentzau' of the publishing business: a promoter and operative of great ingenuity and not much principle' by John Carter, and as much worse by Sadleir 'a manufacturer of novels'.[2] On the other hand, John Sutherland has sought to retrieve his reputation, seeing him as an outsider in a publishing world seeking to be 'dynastic'.[3] By the beginning of the century, for example, Longman had been in business since 1724 and Murray from 1768. Colburn, a newcomer in 1814, noted the leisure of the wealthy and the increase in library readers and set about catering for it with his three-volume fashionable novels. Referred to as the 'Prince of Puffers', his own *New Monthly Magazine* advertised and 'puffed' his own titles.[4]

Sutherland points out that between 1814 and 1824 Colburn published 135 new titles and that 'in his heyday' between 1825 and 1829 (when he sold his library to Saunders and Otley he published 197 titles of which 107 were fiction and 80 three-volume novels.[5]

The recollections of one of the *New Monthly*'s editors provides a contrast to Sadleir's view: Colburn was a little bustling man, who seemed incapable of decision concerning anything — from the choice of a proffered book to the quantity of sugar he should put into his teacup. There was lamentable hesitation in all he did or said, seldom uttering more than half a sentence, and leaving it uncertain what he thought. Yet he was a man of a kindly and generous nature; his impulses were good, and he was considerate and liberal to authors. He was publisher of many of the best works of the time, especially in fiction, both previously to his partnership with Bentley and after the termination of their alliance.[6]

It may not be too fanciful to suppose that Colburn and Disraeli recognized each other as outsiders within their respective hierarchical societies, but perhaps Colburn suited Disraeli's attitude to fiction – something to be exploited when debts were pressing (as well as an outlet for the imagination). Disraeli, twenty-one when *Vivian Grey* was published, was already heavily in debt, a state which was to be more or less permanent for a large part of his life. Debt was to be the main spur (but not the only reason) for much of his literary output. By the time Colburn agreed to publish *Vivian Grey* in 1826, Colburn had already proved the success of the three-volume fashionable novel. He paid Disraeli £200 for the copyright and £500 for his next novel.

Vivian Grey was published anonymously in two volumes. Colburn's experience in 'puffing' had its effect. The novel was widely reviewed and read within 'society', but when the name of the author leaked out Disraeli paid the price of Colburn's advertising. Both reviewers and readers turned on him. Colburn by contrast cannot have complained – he had created another success; by July *Vivian Grey* went into a second edition and in 1827 Part II was published, for which Colburn paid £500.

In 1828 Colburn published Bulwer's *Pelham* (the success of which Disraeli cannot have failed to note). By 1829 Colburn was 'far and away the most successful trade publisher in England'.[7] Disraeli was in successful company which, if attacked by the high-minded, nevertheless had an appreciative market.

Colburn was however in financial difficulties; probably now in his early thirties, the years 1826–7 had been difficult for the publishing industry. Sadleir notes that those years 'swept away two-thirds of the publishing houses of the time'.[8] It is probable that Colburn owed Bentley money and the only way of retrieving it was for Bentley to take a share in Colburn's business in 1829.[9]

Sadleir described Colburn as 'the first of the gambling publishers'. He is compared with Bentley who was everything that Colburn was not: he was a serious-minded craftsman-booklover. To practical ability and knowledge of manufacture, he added an innate, though rather bourgeois, sense of the dignity of a publisher's calling.

Colburn's character on the other hand was one which might have appealed more to the young, ambitious Disraeli: he had no literary taste of his own, merely an instinctive sense of the taste of the moment. In consequence (being incapable of building up a list of permanent saleability) he published on the basis of quick turn-over, and made a fortune for himself by sheer topical ingenuity. His imprint died with him. Not, however, his influence on the trade. Impervious to snubs; cheerful under vilification, so long as insults meant more business; thinking in hundreds where others thought in tens. Colburn revolutionised publishing in its every aspect. He would invent a book which he judged likely to be popular, choose his author and offer a sudden dazzling fee for the copyright. His servility was as calculated as his generosity. He developed advertising, both direct and indirect to a degree hitherto undreamt of.[10]

Advertising, and lots of it, was one of the main characteristics of Colburn, and then of Colburn and Bentley. Colburn and Bentley were reputed to have laid out £27,000 in advertising during the three years of their partnership. Since the firm published 149 ordinary books and forty-six titles in the cheap series within this period, the average cost of advertising each was almost £140.[11]

The partnership with Richard Bentley was not a happy one; Colburn's financial dealings led to quarrels and they parted in 1832.[12] It was nevertheless innovative in its publishing and had a wider influence. This short period coincided with the years prior to the Reform Bill when the market was again slow for fiction publishers. Colburn and Bentley were only two of a new kind of publisher entering the market. In contrast, the (already) older firms for example those of Longman, Murray and Macmillan did not consider fiction to be part of their staple earners.[13]

When Colburn reappeared in 1836 he set up business in Great Marlborough Street.[14] Now the rival of Bentley, who had all Colburn's old authors and most of his copyrights, Colburn secured the publishing rights to Disraeli's two new novels in 1837, a triumph. Sutherland points out that Disraeli is the one 'undoubted first-league author consistently in his [Colburn's] post-partnership list'.[15]

Subsequently Colburn got *Coningsby* (published in May, 1844), of which three editions were sold in as many months, and was again the publisher a year later for *Sybil* (1845), which was almost as successful as *Coningsby*. Both novels were published on a shared profit basis, Disraeli's earnings being about £1,000 in each case. *Tancred* (1847) for which Disraeli earned about £750, was less successful. Blake points out that it was not until *Lothair* and *Endymion* were published that he enjoyed real success. Novels written by an ex-Prime Minister were bound to create a stir.[16]

By the end of 1829 Disraeli had sufficiently recovered to contemplate his desire to journey to the East. He had however reached the limits of his borrowing from his father, when he wrote his much-quoted letter to Benjamin Austen:[17]

> … go I must, tho' I fear I must hack for it. A literary prostitute I have never yet been, tho' born in an age of general prostitution, and tho' I have more than once been subject to temptations which might have been the ruination of a less virtuous young woman. My muse however is still a virgin, but the mystical flower, I fear, must soon be plucked. Colburn I suppose will be the bawd. Tempting Mother Colburn! However…I may yet be saved…[18]

On 14 February 1830 Disraeli wrote to Colburn, with an eye for the market, to tell him about his new novel:

> … I have been fool enough to be intent upon a novel – but such a novel! It will astound you, draw tears from Princesses, and grins from Printers devils: it will atone for all the stupid books you have been lately publishing, and allow me to die in a blaze. In a word to give you an idea of it. It is exactly the kind of work which you wo[ul]d write yourself, if you had time, and delightfully adapted to the most corrupt taste. This immortal work which will set all Europe afire and not be forgotten till at least 3 months has only one fault – it is not written…[19]

By March 1830 *The Young Duke* was finished but Disraeli still hankered after a rapprochement with Murray. He declined to see Disraeli, offering only to look at the manuscript if it were to be delivered to Albemarle Street. Before he left England Disraeli was anxious to ensure that Murray did not misunderstand his decision to go to Colburn after Murray's cool, but not entirely hostile, reply. Murray's publishing is clearly in a different class to Colburn's:

> … As you forced me to decide, I decided as I thought most prudently. The work is one which I dare say, wo[u]d neither disgrace you to publish, nor me to write, but it is not the kind of production, which should recommence our connection, or be introduced to the world by the publisher of Byron …[20]

Colburn eventually published *The Young Duke*, but not until April 1831, a year after he received it. After his return to England, and again sorely in need of money, Disraeli was most anxious not to be tied to Colburn, presumably realizing that prestige lay elsewhere, if his writing was to be taken with the seriousness he wanted – he regarded *Contarini Fleming* as something rather different to anything he had undertaken in the past.[21] He had now, moreover, the slight chance of an opening with Murray.

He offered him *A Psychological Romance*. By 4 March, Murray had made his offer. He agreed to publish the new novel providing Disraeli altered the title to *Contarini Fleming, A Psychological Auto-biography,* but offered only an agreement based on the division of profits.[22] This was far safer from his cautious point of view (the trade was still slow) than an initial outlay for the copyright for which Disraeli had hoped.[23]

Publisher and author each received a profit of £18.[24] Murray's caution was justified and Disraeli ceased for the time being to see himself as a potential author of 'literary' novels; his previous ones had been classed as 'fashionable'. Colburn & Bentley, not Murray, appeared to be his natural publisher.

Once bitten, Murray turned down his next book, *Alroy*, but by 12 January 1833 Disraeli had found a new publisher. Colburn's partnership with Bentley had broken up, with Bentley becoming sole owner – Disraeli had to look elsewhere. And Saunders & Otley (Colburn's rivals, who having bought Colburn's original business, the Conduit Street Library, in 1824/5 then themselves concentrated on publishing three-volume novels for the circulating libraries) offered Disraeli £300 for an edition of 1,000. Writing to Sarah he told her that he had

> … Made an excellent arrangement with S and O. who 'out of sight' are the best fellows I ever dealt with. An edition of only one thousand and a bill at very short date of £300, as much as Bentley wo[ul]d have given me for the copyright, and a thousand apologies in addition for the badness of the times and the lowness of their offer, which in truth is two 3rds of the profits. The fact is they are longsighted fellows and do not care for a miserable immediate profit. They seem quite beside themselves with the connection, and assure me they can sell much more of a book than any other house.[25]

Out with the old and in with the new. Disraeli had been sought after for himself and it must have been flattering after his inability to re-establish a satisfactory relationship with Murray.

Alroy's reception was mostly but not all kind. Five hundred of the initial print run was subscribed before publication.[26] By January 1834 Disraeli had revised his opinion of Saunders and Otley. Writing to Sarah he fumed, 'I am in the greatest rage with S and O. They have no opinion of the work [probably *A Year at Hartlebury*, written with her] at all but especially the second volume. All the Election part they think most weak. I longed to tell them that I wrote it.'[27]

The following month Disraeli used his connection with his father's publisher Edward Moxon (1801–1858), as he had done with Murray, to arrange with him to publish his *Revolutionary Epick*.[28]

In 1836 Disraeli's debts again drove him back to fiction and this time, he approached Colburn, now back in business, who agreed to take two novels. As with any book, reputations and financial interests were at stake but the personal situations of both author and publisher sharpened the necessity for success. Colburn clearly wanted – and needed – him: he had not lost his touch. He wanted to make the most of Disraeli's satirical portraits, encouraging their appearance. He told Disraeli that he hoped 'you will have a dozen more originals to draw from beside old Lady C[ork]; an exhibition of two or three leading political characters would not be amiss'.[29] In May 1837 Colburn published the second three-volume novel, *Venetia*, 'by the author of *Vivian Grey* and *Henrietta Temple*', to favourable reviews and no sooner was it published than he was asking Disraeli for another.

In 1841 after he was returned to Parliament for Shrewsbury, Disraeli started to create a new identity for himself; eschewing the 'dandified' image he had previously cultivated, he began to appear more soberly dressed and more 'positive about his Jewishness…developing a theory of Jewish superiority turning his chief political liability into an asset'.[30]

This change was reflected in his new novel which he started in September 1843. It was to be the first book of a trilogy which was quite different in nature to his previous novels. In March 1844 Colburn published *Coningsby; or, the New Generation*, in three volumes. Its success had Disraeli immediately planning a sequel, which would deal with the 'Condition of England'; in May 1845 Colburn published *Sybil: or, the Two Nations*, also in three volumes for which Colburn paid him £800. Its reception was less enthusiastic than that for *Coningsby* and in the following year, 1847, Colburn published *Tancred: or the New Crusade*. In December 1851, they published Disraeli's biography of his friend, Lord George Bentinck (see No. 64).

By 1852 Colburn's era was passing. Now elderly, he sold his business to Hurst and Blackett.[31] It was time for a change. Disraeli owned his copyrights. When a new publisher approached him in 1864 he was happy to start a new relationship. He published no further novels until 1870, when he was sixty-six, and his next major negotiation with a publisher was not to be until 1864. In 1865 he met Montagu Corry (later Lord Rowton) who as his private secretary from 1866 took a major part in Disraeli's future arrangements with his publisher.[32]

In late nineteenth-century London, Longman remained one of the most important London publishers. When Disraeli first became involved with the firm in May 1864, two Longmans were at its head: Thomas Norton Longman IV (1804–1879) and his younger brother William (1813–1877). As it developed, Disraeli's business relationship with Longman IV, always cordial, became one of genuine respect and friendship.

At their suggestion Longman printed a revised version of Disraeli's *Revolutionary Epick* in May 1864 but by July it was clear they had over-printed: Thomas Longman told Disraeli that he intended to sell off the remaining 556 copies. Disraeli immediately offered to indemnify the publisher but Longman refused to hear of it:

> The accident of life is one of those incidents of trade to which we are liable. Indeed it is one of the grounds on which, what some people have called, the rapacity of publishers is justified. I do not however less highly appreciate the honourable & kind feeling of your proposal.[33]

In 1867 Longman published Disraeli's speeches on Parliamentary Reform, edited by Corry, and in July 1870 arrangements were progressing for the publication of *Lothair* which was published on a royalty basis. Disraeli received '10s on the pound on [sic] all copies sold'.[34] *Lothair* was published in three volumes in May 1870. Its popularity was huge. Longman wrote to Disraeli that 'Mr Mudie's house was in a state of siege'. By 1876 Disraeli had earned over £6,000.[35]

Its success had revived interest in Disraeli's earlier novels and five years later, on 26 January 1877, Longman suggested that his firm should purchase the copyright in all Disraeli's novels for £2000 guineas; 'Our object would be to reproduce them in a cheaper form at 2/- each or 2/6 in a cloth binding, in a series we publish called the "Novelists Library".'[36] On 29 January Disraeli accepted the proposal.[37]

Later that year William Longman died and two years later in 1879, Thomas Longman IV also died, leaving the firm in the hands of his son, the young thirty-year old Thomas Norton Longman V (1849-1930) (see No. 88). In his memoirs, written in 1921, and looking back over a long publishing life (he had entered the Longman partnership in 1873) Longman wrote that perhaps the relationship with Disraeli 'was the most interesting of all my experiences'.[38]

Between June and July Longman negotiated a sum for Disraeli's new novel. Encouraged by the success of Lothair the firm decided that the huge sum of £10,000 was worth the risk. Longman wrote to Rowton confirming their arrangement: £2,500 on delivery of the manuscript and the balance of £7,500 on 1 April 1881. He added that he believed it to be the largest sum ever paid for a work of fiction.[39]

Disraeli wrote that he regarded the offer 'a truly liberal one & I accept it with pleasure, but I would not do so, unless I had a conviction, that you would have no cause to regret the enterprise'.[40] One of the stranger aspects of the agreement (less so today) is that neither Longman nor Rowton had seen a word of the manuscript.[41]

Disraeli invited Longman to Hughenden in August 1880 and in a pencilled note now attached to Rowton's letter of 11 August Longman listed the names of those represented in *Endymion*: 'Lord Lyndhurst/ Lord Rothschild/ George Smyth/ Lady Jersey/ Lord Cockburn/ Himself/ Lord Hertford'.[42]

Endymion was published at a moment when discussion in the press and among publishers was at its height over the stranglehold the three-volume novel had on fiction publishing, as well as the then current anxieties over copyright and the American market (see No. 126). Deciding which book should be published at 31s 6d for the readership of the circulating libraries, and which published at a low price to attract a general sale, was as important as taking the decision to publish at all. In deciding not only whether but how to publish *Endymion* this aspect was one to which Longman gave much thought.[43] In the event Longman published a three-volume edition in November and a cheap edition hard on its heels in February 1881. It was not the success for which Longman might have hoped, in terms of his outlay, but by 24 March they had sold more than 8,000 copies making, Longman reported, 'a good start'.[44]

On Thursday 19 April at 4.30 am Disraeli died. The limited space in the church was kept for those invited; most of the leading figures of the day were there, and it has been said that no literary figures were invited. Longman's reminiscences of 28 April however prove otherwise and bear testimony to an unusual relationship between an elderly former Prime Minister and a young thirty-year old publisher:

> The sad ceremony I had the honour of attending the day before yesterday will for ever live in the memory of all who were present. Nothing could have been more simple in its character, nothing more striking in its solemnity, and nothing more strictly in accordance with his wishes. I may well say I shall not forget so great an occasion, not only from the fact that the ceremony was the burial of a great man, but from the very select band of followers I had the privilege of joining. There were only 110 invitations sent out, and all these were not made use of.[45]

Annabel Jones

1   Michael Sadleir, *XIX Century Fiction: A Bibliographical Record based on his own Collection*, 2 vols. (London and Berkeley, 1951), II. 112–13, and John Sutherland, 'Henry Colburn Publisher', *Publishing History*, 19 (1986), 59–84.

2   *Victorian Fiction: an Exhibition of Original Editions, January – February 1947*, arranged by John Carter with the collaboration of Michael Sadleir (London [Published for the National Book League by the Cambridge University Press], 1947).

3   Sutherland, 'Henry Colburn Publisher', 59–84.

4   Ibid., 81.

5   Ibid., 69. Writing a century later in his *Memoirs* (unpublished) Thomas Norton Longman V commented that 'one of the greatest problems a publisher has to solve is how best to make his books known … his object is the same as that of any other man of business…to make as much as he can out of the trade he conducts!' (*Memoirs*, Vol. 1 (1921), pp. 21-22).

6   S.C. Hall, *Retrospect of a Long Life: From 1815 to 1833* (London, 1883), 2 vols., I. 316.

7   Sutherland, 'Henry Colburn Publisher', 70-71.

8   John Sutherland, in *Victorian Novelists and Publishers* (Chicago, 1978), drawing on Mrs Oliphant's *Annals of a Publishing House*, describes Constable and Ballantyne's bankruptcy in 1826 as a 'terrible precedent'. 'For a while

afterwards the banks would not change the bills of any bookseller and the whole publishing industry quaked. Even Longman's with a hundred years of prosperous trading behind them were rumoured to be at risk.'

9   Sadleir, *XIX Century Fiction*, II. 112-13.

10   Ibid.

11   See R. A. Gettman, *A Victorian Publisher, The Study of the Bentley Papers* (Cambridge, 1960), p. 122; he quotes John Chapman's *Cheap Books and How to Get Them* (London, 1852).

12   Gettman, *A Victorian Publisher*, pp. 15-20

13   In February 1831 Colburn and Bentley started their series of Standard Novels. These were one-volume novels at six shillings, reprints of three- (or two-) volume original editions priced at 31s 6d. Suddenly fiction was within the reach of the 'prosperous artisan or clerk', providing a new market for hard-pressed publishers, reluctant to invest in new copyrights and expensive original editions at a time of political upheaval. Richard D. Altick, *The English Common Reader: A Social History of the Mass Reading Public, 1800-1900* (Chicago, 1957), p. 274.

14   Gettman, *A Victorian Publisher*, pp. 20-21.

15   Sutherland, 'Henry Colburn Publisher', p. 76.

16   Robert Blake, *Disraeli* (London, 1966; rpt. 1969), pp. 192-3.

17   Jane Ridley, *The Young Disraeli* (London, 1995), p. 71.

18   J.A.W. Gunn, John Matthews, Donald M. Schurman, M.G. Wiebe (eds.), *Benjamin Disraeli Letters Volume I: 1815–1834* (Toronto, 1982), p. 74: Disraeli to Benjamin Austen, 8 December 1829.

19   *Disraeli Letters I*, p. 76: Disraeli to Henry Colburn, 14 February 1830.

20   *Disraeli Letters I*, p. 86: Disraeli to John Murray, 27 May 1830.

21   Ridley, *Young Disraeli*, p. 104.

22   *Disraeli Letters I*, p. 155: Disraeli to John Murray, 19 March 1832.

23   Ridley, *Young Disraeli*, p. 108.

24   See Ridley, *Young Disraeli*, p. 115, n. 43.

25   *Disraeli Letters I*, p. 228: Disraeli to Sarah D'Israeli, 12 January 1833.

26   Ridley, *Young Disraeli*, p. 129.

27   *Disraeli Letters I*, p. 306: Disraeli to Sarah D'Israeli, 31 December 1833.

28   *Disraeli Letters I*, p. 310: Disareli to Edward Moxon, 24[?]February 1834. Moxon, a publisher of some experience, had worked for Longman between 1821 and 1827, when he left eventually to set up on his own in 1830. He published Isaac D'Israeli's *The Genius of Judaism* in 1833 and in 1834 was arranging to publish his *Curiosities of Literature*. The *Dictionary of National Biography* notes that he told Charles Grenville in 1847 that Disraeli had asked to enter into partnership with him but he refused 'not thinking that he was prudent enough to be trusted'.

29   Matthew Whiting Ross, *The Silver Fork School* (N.Y., 1936) p. 200, quoted in Gettman, *Victorian Publisher*, p. 63.

30   Ridley, *Young Disraeli*, p. 256.

31   Sutherland, 'Henry Colburn Publisher', p. 78.

32   Blake, *Disraeli*, pp. 412-3.

33   Dep. Hughenden 235/1, fol. 11

34   Guinevere L. Griest, *Mudie's Circulating Library and the Victorian Novel* (Newton Abbot, 1970), p. 200.

35   Blake, *Disraeli*, p. 519.

36   Dep. Hughenden 235/1, fol. 203.

37   Longman Archives/Beaconsfield Correspondence /4.

38   *Memories Personal and Various*, For Personal Circulation Thomas Norton Longman, 1921 (unpublished).

39   Dep. Hughenden 235/2, fols. 87-8.

40   Longman Archives /Beaconsfield Correspondence 8.

41   W.F. Monypenny and G.E. Buckle, *Life of Benjamin Disraeli*, 6 vols. (London, 1910-20), VI. p. 551. There is perhaps a nice irony in the fact that the house of John Murray was the publisher of Disraeli's *Life*.

42   University of Reading /Longman Archives: Beaconsfield Correspondence /7.

43   For a detailed account of the publication of *Endymion* see Annabel Jones, '*Endymion*: A Case Study in Nineteenth Century Publishing', MA Thesis, University of Leicester 1972, and a shortened published version in Asa Briggs, *Essays in the History of Publishing*, (London, 1974), pp. 143-86.

44   See Jones, '*Endymion*: A Case Study', pp. 70-72.

45   *Memories* Chapter IV p. 110; letter to Henry Reeve.

Disraeli's Novels and the Beckford Connection

WITH THE publication in 1833 of *The Wondrous Tale of Alroy*, Disraeli had completed a triptych of novels in which he explored his own nature and possible future career. As he commented: 'In Vivian Grey I have pourtrayed my active and real ambition. In *Alroy*, my ideal ambition. The P.R. [*Contarini Fleming: A Psychological Romance*] is a developmt. of my poetic character. This trilogy is the secret history of my feelings – I shall write no more about myself.'[1] To explore his 'poetic character' Disraeli believed that it would be essential to write in the first person and to choose a character close to his own, but 'whose position in life should be at variance, and, as it were, in constant conflict with his temperament; and the accidents of whose birth, nevertheless, tended to develop his psychology'.[2]

As a novelist Disraeli was always more ready to cannibalize a real person than to invent a character from scratch. Count Mirabel in *Henrietta Temple* is based on the French dandy, Count D'Orsay. Lord Cadurcis and Marmion Herbert in *Venetia* on Lord Byron and Shelley. As the model for an analysis of his own 'poetic character' Disraeli daringly chose William Beckford,

the notorious author of *Vathek* and immensely rich builder of Fonthill Abbey. He rearranged the details of Beckford's life to fit a half German, half Italian central figure, Contarini Fleming, and was so pleased with the result that he sent a copy of the book to his model, like some literary scalp.[3]

Beckford received the unsolicited tribute with unreserved rapture, writing in a draft reply: 'How wildly original! How full of intense thought! How startling! How delightful!', but then changed in the actual letter 'startling' to 'awakening'.[4] The word switch was significant. In May 1832 Beckford was seventy-one years old, forty more than his admirer.

Fig. 2 **William Beckford** (1760-1844) by C. F. Tayler. Photograph of painting reproduced with permission of Victoria Art Gallery, Bath and North East Somerset Council.

Fig. 3 **The Lansdown Tower**, from Willes Maddox's *Views of Lansdown Tower*
Photograph reproduced with permission of Bristol University Special Collections.

He had fallen into a low, predictable routine in his Bath home in Lansdown Crescent, arranging flowers, rearranging the art collection in the tower which he had built on the hill above the Crescent, and proposing spiteful little books that no one wanted to publish. *Contarini Fleming* roused him from a negative old age into a new burst of successful publications.

The novel is one of flashy brilliance and glib profundity. To analyze his own poetic character, which never matured beyond florid, aureate prose, Disraeli had chosen a man whose own published writing had also hovered on the edge of poetry without ever toppling over into it. By 1832 Beckford had still not outlived the paedophile scandal of his youth, when he had chosen Swiss exile rather than face up to accusations of seducing the eleven-year-old Lord William Courtenay.[5] With remarkable courage, considering his own enigmatic sexual identity, Disraeli did not underplay this aspect of Contarini Fleming-Beckford. It is evident from the detailed portrait of Contarini that, though Disraeli wrote the book on a slow passage from Egypt, he had previously put in much time researching Beckford's idiosyncrasies and his past life.

As Beckford had a private devotion to St Anthony, so Contarini, who is the son, like Beckford, of a successful politician, secretly worships Mary Magdalen. Sent to school he meets his Courtenay, a boy called Musaeus, and the romance is described with an uninhibited gusto suggesting that Disraeli believed such sexual freedom to be an inherent part of the 'poetic character':

> I never beheld so lovely and so pensive a countenance…rich brown curls clustered in hyacinthine grace upon the delicate rose of his downy cheek… I loved him. My friendship was a passion…Oh! days of rare and pure felicity, when Musaeus and myself, with our arms around each other's neck, wandered together amid the meads…I forced him to assure me, in a voice of agitation, that he loved me alone. [6]

Beckford is likely to have been moved by such an open recall of his own past. As arrogant, aristocratic and bad tempered as his model, Contarini presses on, writes, anonymously like Beckford's *Vathek*, a brilliant novel, *Manstein*, then settles in Switzerland, but courts a cousin-bride melodramatically in Venice. She dies in childbirth like Beckford's young wife. A richly over-written travelogue follows, around the shores of the Mediterranean where Disraeli had recently been adventuring. What particularly caught Beckford's eye was the exuberant style of this travel section. Disraeli's brazen impudence claiming that such poetic prose was superior to rhyme and metre would have been most encouraging.[7]

All his adult life Beckford had had an obsession with building towers so, as a last and most winning stroke in the book, Contarini settles down and builds a tower, five feet higher than the one Beckford had recently built on Lansdown, but in Naples, not Bath. Copying Beckford's other obsession with being buried above ground to escape the worms, Contarini vows: 'This tower I shall dedicate to the Future, and I intend that it shall be my tomb…. Here let me pass my life in the study and the creation of the beautiful.'[8]

It was exactly the inspiration that Beckford needed and he promptly set to work on his own 'creation of the beautiful'. Disraeli continued to pay court, but there was still no meeting. Then, in March 1833, he sent Beckford a copy of his next and most exotic novel, *The Wondrous Tale of Alroy*. If the old man had been flattered by *Contarini Fleming* he was captivated by *Alroy*. He wrote to his bookseller, George Clarke, not to Disraeli, 'I have slowly and reluctantly finished the truly wondrous tale of Alroy, which I wish had been extended to 20 volumes. I did not hurry on, fearful of expending the treasure too fast, for a treasure I consider it to be, and of the richest kind.'[9] *Contarini* had been an unauthorised raid on his life story, but *Alroy* was, he believed, the true child of his *Vathek*, an acknowledgement of his own picaresque genius: 'The halls of Eblis, the thrones of the Solimans are for ever present in his mind's eye, tinted with somewhat different hues from those of the original; but pertaining of the same awful and dire solemnity.'[10] Knowing that Disraeli was a heavy smoker, Beckford, who hated tobacco smoke, had been avoiding a personal encounter with his young admirer. *Alroy* changed his mind, if only for a day or two. 'I will appear to him the very first opportunity,' he told his bookseller.[11] Clarke had been sounding out the possibilities and reported that Disraeli was the most conceited person he had ever met and an 'Oriental Voluptuary'.[12]

Beckford had been given all the encouragement he needed. In his papers he already had a travel journal of real distinction, an honest vulnerable account in sensitive prose of his year of exile in Portugal back in 1787–8. At that time the country had been a crumbling Catholic Ruritania where he had been obliged to act dextrously in response to a complex diplomatic impasse. Unfortunately for his reputation the Journal would have to wait for publication until the twentieth century. Instead, impressed by Disraeli's fine writing, he completely re-orchestrated the text with a number of riotous set-piece incidents that had never happened and meetings with Portuguese royalty that had never taken place, all written with an airy confidence quite unlike the nervous, tentative tone of the real Journal. He called it *Italy; with Sketches of Spain and Portugal*, and it was published, to excellent reviews, in 1834. French and American editions followed.

The two writers finally met on 12 June 1834 at a performance of Rossini's *Semiramide* in London's King's Theatre. The evening was a moderate success. Beckford boasted about his ability to read a music score and spot a picture restoration on sight. For his part Disraeli was impressed. 'I have had three interviews of late', he told his sister, 'with three remarkable men who fill the public ear at present; O'Connell; Beckford; and Lord Durham. The first is the man of the greatest genius; the second of the greatest taste; and the last of the greatest ambition'.[13] The next day he sent Beckford 'a piece of marble which I myself brought from the Parthenon' to use as a bookend with a plea for continued contact, but they never met again though they continued a correspondence of mutual admiration for another five years.[14]

In 1835 *Recollections of an Excursion to the Monasteries of Alcobaça and Batalha* was published. Beckford was taking seriously the advice that the Chevalier de Winter, Contarini Fleming's artist guru, gives: 'Create. Man is made to create, from the poet to the potter'.[15] The *Recollections* are a return to the light whimsicalities of the Journal, a compression of several Portuguese journeys into one happy twelve-day excursion, made in the company of two old clergymen, to monasteries little changed from their romantic medieval social order. The book ends hauntingly with the mad Queen Maria of Portugal wailing, 'Ai Jesous! Ai Jesous!' in the darkness of her palace of Queluz, where Beckford was advising the Prince Regent: a most telling imaginative invention.

For Disraeli the Beckford influence had preceded the meeting by several years. *Alroy* had been begun in 1830 and revitalised by the author's visit to Jerusalem. As a representation of his 'ideal ambition' it is a remarkably revealing text. Its hero, a twelfth-century Jewish prince from the

Caucasus, ends by having his head cut off in a public square in Baghdad; his last triumph being the mocking smile still fixed upon that severed member because he has contrived to infuriate his conqueror, Alp Arslan, King of Karasmé, so much that he has escaped a promised death by slow torture.

The book is a serious historical romance. Prince David Alroy rallies the Jews of Kurdistan to defeat the Arabs, overwhelm Iraq and take Baghdad. But instead of pressing on to Jerusalem he marries the Caliph's wicked daughter, Princess Schirene, a Muslim. She betrays him, he refuses to renounce his faith and taunts his captor by claiming immortality. This claim is promptly put to the test by Alp Arslan's sabre, with a predictable result. *Alroy* is an impressive anticipation of Zionism, the Balfour Declaration and the modern state of Israel. It is also an intriguing sidelight on Disraeli's hidden loyalties and dreams. Beckford was right to claim the influence of his own novel, *Vathek*. Disraeli has borrowed *Vathek*'s frequent sorties into magic realism with long footnotes by the author to explain any episodes of cabalistic significance. To fight victoriously Alroy must receive the sceptre of Solomon from that king's own hands and to do so must enter a subterranean chamber, one clearly inspired by Vathek's Hall of Eblis, where the dead kings sit:

> The portal opened with a crash of thunder louder than an earthquake. Pale, panting, and staggering, the Prince of the Captivity entered an illimitable hall, illumined by pendulous balls of glowing metal. On each side of the hall, sitting on golden thrones, was ranged a line of kings, and, as the pilgrim entered, the monarchs rose, and took off their diadems, and waved them thrice, and thrice repeated, in solemn chorus: 'All hail Alroy! Hail to thee, brother king! Thy crown awaits thee!'[16]

Prose-poetry of dubious merit is employed to enrich passages of pseudo-oriental magnificence:

> The household of Alroy and Schirene. Foremost, the Lord Honain riding upon a chestnut charger, shod with silver; the dress of the rider, pink with silver stars. From his rosy turban depended a tremulous aigrette of brilliants, blazing with a thousand shifting tints. Two hundred pages followed him; and then servants of both sexes, gorgeously habited, amounting to nearly two thousand, carrying rich vases, magnificent caskets, and costly robes. The treasurer and two hundred of his underlings came next, showering golden dirhems on all sides. The sceptre of Solomon borne by Asriel himself.[17]

Most Beckfordian of all is the swaggering tone of doomed arrogance that pervades the narrative. Disraeli was on course to set off a train of British, not Jewish, imperial pomps, which would only end in the twenty-first century when a crown, with the Kohinoor diamond glittering on its band, was carried down the aisle of Westminster Abbey on the coffin of Elizabeth, the last Empress of India, that title of Beckfordian grandiosity which Disraeli had devised to flatter his dumpy Queen.

Timothy Mowl

1   J. A. W. Gunn, John Matthews, Donald M. Schurman, M. G. Wiebe (eds.), *Benjamin Disraeli Letters Volume I: 1815–1834* (Toronto, 1982), 'The Mutilated Diary', p. 447.
2   Preface to the 1845 edition of *Contarini Fleming* (London, 1832; rpt. 1927), p. x.
3   He wrote in his 'Mutilated Diary': 'I shall always consider "the Psych" as the perfection of English Prose'; quoted in *Disraeli Letters 1*, p. 447.
4   Bodleian Library, Oxford, MS. Beckford c.14, fols. 69-70. Disraeli mentions Beckford's enthusiasm in a letter to Sarah D'Israeli of 26 May 1832: J. A. W. Gunn, John Matthews, Donald M. Schurman, M. G. Wiebe (eds.), *Benjamin Disraeli Letters Volume I: 1815–1834* (Toronto, 1982), p. 280.
5   Timothy Mowl, *William Beckford: Composing for Mozart* (London, 1998), pp. 103–12.
6   *Contarini Fleming*, pp. 24–7.
7   Beckford had written a fine prose-poem himself, 'The Satyr's Range' (MS. Beckford c. 47).
8   *Contarini Fleming*, p. 363.
9   *Disraeli Letters I*, p. 340, fn. 2: Disraeli to Sarah Austen, 16 March 1833.
10 R. J. Gemmett (ed.), *The Consummate Collector: William Beckford's Letters to his Bookseller* (Norwich, 2000), p. 186; quoted in Jerry Nolan, 'Brief Encounter of Beckford and Disraeli, or The Radical Pair of "Oriental Voluptuaries"', *The Beckford Journal*, 8 (2002), 66–78 (69).
11 Nolan, 'Brief Encounter', 69.
12 Ibid., 68.
13 *Disraeli Letters 1*, p. 412: Disraeli to Sarah D'Israeli, 16 June 1834.
14 Ibid., p. 410: Disraeli to Beckford, 13 June 1834.
15 *Contarini Fleming*, p. 361.
16 *Alroy* (London, 1833; rpt. 1927), p. 95.
17 Ibid., p. 174.

Disraeli and Buckinghamshire

BENJAMIN DISRAELI has been regarded as an essentially urban, cosmopolitan and un-English figure. Robert Blake asserted that Disraeli was 'the least English of Englishmen' and many historians have emphasized Disraeli's Jewishness.[1] Disraeli was certainly proud of his Jewish ancestry, but he was baptized as an Anglican at the age of twelve and he spent most of his adult life in gentile society. Disraeli was English, not only by religion, but also by background and outlook. He was a third generation Englishman on his father's side and a fifth generation Englishman on his mother's side and he always regarded himself as English. In 1832 he wrote: 'My politics are described by one word, and that word is England.'[2] Disraeli asserted his Englishness, not just in public, but also in private when it brought him no political advantage. In 1826, after a tour of France and Italy, he told his father: 'I feel now that it is not prejudice, when I declare that England with all her imperfections is worth all the world together.'[3] After 1845 Disraeli went abroad only twice: to Paris in 1856 and to Berlin (for the Congress) in 1878. He spent most of his time away from Westminster in his rural home, high up in the Chiltern hills in Buckinghamshire.

Disraeli first became familiar with the Buckinghamshire Chilterns in 1825 when his literary father, Isaac, rented Hyde House, near Amersham. Four years later, in 1829, Isaac leased the 1,351 acre Bradenham Manor estate, near High Wycombe and settled his family there (see No. 17). The move was partly prompted by a serious breakdown in Benjamin's physical and mental health.[4] He found the solitude and silence of the countryside more endurable than life in London and quickly fell in love with what he called 'our beloved and beechy Bucks'.[5]

At Bradenham, the Disraeli family – including Benjamin's beloved sister, Sarah, and his younger brothers, James and Ralph – lived a comfortable, but reclusive rural life. In his last novel, *Endymion*, Benjamin described his family's life at Bradenham in the 1830s. He recalled that 'their communications with the outer world were slight and rare' and that they were 'morally, as well as materially, *adscripti glebae*'.[6] Bradenham was certainly inaccessible at that time because it was far from a railway station and the roads to it were often blocked in winter by drifting snow. This suited Disraeli because it enabled him to escape from what he called 'the plague of women, the wear and tear of politics and the dunning of creditors'.[7] Until his election to Parliament and marriage in the late 1830s, he lived in fear of being arrested for debts accumulated in London by rash speculations in bubble shares and publishing ventures. He wanted to make a fresh start in the country and begged his solicitor to 'preserve me from a Sheriff's officer in my own county'.[8]

Fig .4 **Hughenden Manor**. Pen drawing by R. Green, 1840; reproduced by permission of Hughenden Manor (The National Trust). This romantic view shows the house before it was remodelled by Lamb (see No. 57).

During his first decade in Parliament Disraeli represented two constituencies far from Bucks: Maidstone and Shrewsbury. But he spent most of the long parliamentary recess – from August to January – at Bradenham. There he made good use of his father's library of 25,000 volumes and wrote much including most of his two novels, *Coningsby* and *Tancred*. The isolation of Bradenham enabled him to concentrate on his writing – which boosted his reputation and finances – but provided him with few opportunities for socializing. Nevertheless he observed that 'after a quarantine of a fortnight or so, I get seasoned … and it seems impossible that I ever could live anywhere except among the woods and turfy wildernesses of this dear county'.[9] Even when Disraeli was in London, pursuing his political career, he showed a keen interest in affairs at Bradenham, such as the state of the corn harvest.[10] Wheat was the principal local crop at that time and Disraeli described Wycombe as 'the greatest corn market in England'.[11] Thus his residence at Bradenham encouraged him to support the preservation of the Corn Laws.

Despite Disraeli's affection for Bradenham, it has been claimed that he remained 'in temperament, in consciousness, in aspect … a stranger and a sojourner' there.[12] Yet he always left Bradenham with reluctance: 'I never leave home without feeling as I did when I went to school'.[13] He was, however, a sojourner there in the sense that he had no long-term future on an estate which was only leased by his father. As early as 1829, Disraeli yearned for a permanent Bucks estate of his own but his father refused to help him buy one.[14] In 1837 he wanted to purchase Chequers Court (which later became the country home of the Prime Minister) and in 1843 he tried, unsuccessfully, to buy the Addington estate, north of Aylesbury.[15] In 1846 Disraeli began negotiations to buy the 750 acre Hughenden Manor estate which was over the hill from Bradenham. The sale was agreed in 1847 – for a purchase price of £34,950 – but was not completed until 1848, when Isaac bought the property on his son's behalf. The purchase was assisted by a large loan from the wealthy Bentinck family.

Disraeli engaged an architect, E. B. Lamb, who gave the house a mock-Jacobean frontage, a library and a park (*see* No. 57).[16] The latter additions reflected Disraeli's lifelong passion for books and trees. When he returned to Hughenden he always spent the first week examining the trees in the park and the books in the library.[17] Hughenden, like Bradenham, was over 400 feet up in the Chilterns, so the air was pure and the land well drained – an important consideration for Disraeli who suffered from poor health and respiratory disease for most of his life. Although the poor state of his health and finances precluded him from hunting or shooting, in other ways he behaved like a typical Victorian country gentleman. When walking around his estate or attending local agricultural meetings he dressed in country fashion – wearing a billycock hat and leather gaiters.[18] He regularly visited his tenants and took a solicitous interest in their health and welfare.[19] He also spent much money on improving and extending his estate. On a visit to Hughenden, in 1869, Lord Stanley wrote: 'Cottages much improved: D. is doing them up one by one, and spends, he tells me, all the rental of the estate upon it'. He also noted that Disraeli had made several recent purchases so that Hughenden was now a compact estate of 1,200 acres.[20] Disraeli was a typical squire in a religious sense as well. He received the Sacrament every Easter at Hughenden Church and was on good terms with the Anglican clergy in the diocese. He also helped to revive the local harvest festival.[21]

Like many other Victorian squires, Disraeli became an active county magistrate. He was appointed to the Buckinghamshire bench in 1836 – before he became an MP – and for many years he attended both the petty sessions at West Wycombe and the quarter sessions at Aylesbury.[22] As a Justice of the Peace, he opposed Whig proposals for elected county government and stipendiary magistrates on the grounds that they undermined local autonomy.[23] When Disraeli became an MP he described the House of Commons as 'something like Quarter Sessions on a great scale'.[24] In his famous 1846 speech opposing the repeal of the Corn Laws, he claimed that the British ex-patriot 'riding on elephants, surrounded by slaves ... is always dreaming of quarter sessions'.[25] He compared the Bucks quarter sessions at Aylesbury with 'the old assembling of the Estates of a Province, with the Governor, or Lord Lieutenant, in the chair, and all the notables around him'.[26] In 1856 Disraeli became chairman of a quarter sessions committee to deal with the new County Police Act, which obliged him to be 'as busy this autumn as if I were in the House of Commons'.[27]

For nearly thirty years – from 1847 until 1876 – Disraeli was a knight of the shire for Buckinghamshire. He considered that his election as a county MP was 'the event of my public life which has given me the greatest satisfaction'.[28] But when he first put himself forward as a candidate for the county, in 1832, his dandified dress, shoulder length curly hair and eccentric manner provoked mirth and he was ridiculed as 'the Bradenham braggart' and a Jewish adventurer.[29] Consequently he soon withdrew from the contest, but he remained hopeful that he would eventually represent the county.[30] His chance finally came in 1847, when he was returned as one of two Conservative representatives for the three-seat Buckinghamshire constituency. A member of Disraeli's election committee noted his pride in his adopted county, 'which he regarded as the cradle of most that was good and great in the history of the country'.[31] In his campaign speeches, Disraeli recalled the local connections of past statesmen like Hampden, Shelburne, Burke and Grenville:

> The county of Buckingham has always taken a lead in the political fortunes of this country. ... It gave us the British constitution in the seventeenth century and it created the British Empire in the eighteenth. ... Now let the men of the North, who thought

that they were to govern England – let them bring a political pedigree equal to that of the county of Buckingham.[32]

Disraeli later warned Parliament that 'the blood of those men who refused to pay ship-money is not to be trifled with' – a reference to Hampden and his Bucks supporters in the 1630s.[33] Before his election, Disraeli looked forward to becoming 'the representative of the most essentially agricultural county in England'.[34] But after his election he refused to campaign for the restoration of the corn laws – partly because of the changed sentiments of his county constituents. In 1849 he wrote from Hughenden: 'The cry of Protection will rally no one to our standard here. The farmers think that they have been used as political tools.' He noted that a recent decrease in the local demand for agricultural labour had been offset by an increase in demand for local manufactures like straw plait, lace and chairs.[35] By 1851 local agriculture had also revived and Disraeli wrote to his sister:

> At this moment, with the exception of wheat, all agricultural produce is as high as the average of the last twenty years – ... It is possible that agriculture may flourish without a high price of wheat, and without producing any. There certainly seems to me no reason for its appearance in the Chilterns, unless it fetches a high price. I believe all the farmers in this district who have decent capital are much more than making both ends meet.[36]

Disraeli went to considerable lengths to keep in touch with his Buckinghamshire constituents. The undivided county constituency stretched from the Thames at Eton to the Ouse near Bedford and covered an area of 750 square miles. Disraeli regularly addressed meetings across the county from Slough in the south, to Buckingham and Newport Pagnell in the north. These often involved difficult journeys for him because the county was poorly served by railway lines until after his death. But the Bucks electors repaid Disraeli by returning him to Parliament on eleven occasions. Moreover they only twice put him to the cost and trouble of a contested election – which was a great boon for a relatively poor man with large debts. At his first contest, in 1852, Disraeli received almost as many votes as the Tory who topped the poll – a good result for a man who neither owned a large estate, nor came from an old county family. In 1874 he was surprised and annoyed by 'my *contested!!* election', but he topped the poll and his expenses were paid by his Tory constituents.[37]

In his last novel, Disraeli observed: 'However vast may appear to be the world in which we move, we all of us live in a limited circle. It is the result of circumstances; of our convenience and our taste.'[38] This was certainly true of Disraeli even after he had become the leader of the Conservatives in the House of Commons.

In 1855 the Tory Chief Whip complained that Disraeli associated only 'with his most intimate friends or with his followers and political supporters in Buckinghamshire'.[39] But Disraeli's friends in Bucks helped him with national politics. His trusted solicitor, Philip Rose, who lived at Penn, near Hughenden, was the principal agent of the Conservative party from 1853 until 1859 and one of his private secretaries, Charles Fremantle, came from a leading Buckinghamshire landed family.

Disraeli's long service as a knight of the shire reflected his successful assimilation into Bucks county society. Yet one historian has described him as 'an odd graft upon Buckinghamshire society' while another has claimed that he was not on intimate terms with any of the established county families.[40] This claim seems to be borne out by a comment Disraeli made in 1858 when he was asked for a cadetship by a local gentry family:

> For the Tyrwhitt Drakes to ask a service from me is the Hapsburgs soliciting something from a parvenu Napoleon. After thirty years of scorn and sullenness they have melted before time and events.[41]

This was an exaggeration, however, because the Tyrwhitt Drakes had communicated with Disraeli before he rose to power and they were not in the first rank of Buckinghamshire families.[42] Disraeli, moreover, had been accepted by Bucks county society long before he became a government minister. For example, Sir Harry Verney, a prominent Whig landowner, had written to Disraeli in 1847: 'Few things have occurred in Bucks lately so gratifying to me as your purchase of Hughenden.'[43] From the late 1830s Disraeli was on good terms with the leading Whig landowner in the county, Lord Carrington, who lived at Wycombe Abbey and whom Disraeli described as 'a friend and neighbour'.[44] Carrington had disliked Disraeli's rival candidature to his heir at three Wycombe elections in the early1830s, but in 1838 he invited him to Wycombe Abbey. There Disraeli met two daughters of Lord Forester – the future Ladies Chesterfield and Bradford – who became his closest friends and correspondents in later life. In 1839 Disraeli wrote that Carrington 'talked to me a great deal' and was 'very civil and conservative'.[45] Some years later, Carrington, as Lord Lieutenant of Buckinghamshire, granted Disraeli's request to be made a Deputy Lieutenant for the county.[46]

In the 1830s Disraeli had close political relations with Richard Grenville, the Marquis of Chandos, who was the heir of the first Duke of Buckingham and Chandos. At that time, the Grenvilles were the first family in Buckinghamshire. The first Duke owned nearly 25,000 acres in the county and lived in great state at Stowe, near Buckingham.[47] His son, Chandos, lived at Wotton, the ancestral home of the Grenvilles, which was not far from Bradenham. Chandos was a Buckinghamshire MP and the leader of the Tories in the county. His popularity was largely due to his stalwart defence of the agricultural interest which earned him the title 'the farmer's friend'. Chandos played a crucial role in establishing Disraeli as a figure in both local and national politics.

When Disraeli first stood for Parliament, as an Independent candidate at Wycombe, in 1832, his election agent was an associate of Chandos, which lent credence to Whig claims that he was a Tory in disguise.[48] After a second defeat at Wycombe, in December 1832, Disraeli put himself forward as an anti-Whig candidate for Buckinghamshire, but he soon withdrew and then canvassed for Chandos.[49] In 1833 Disraeli supported the Bucks Agricultural Association, which Chandos had established to represent the local agricultural interest.[50] In 1834 Chandos invited Disraeli to Wotton to discuss politics and thereafter their association was close.[51] Chandos financially assisted Disraeli's Tory candidature at Taunton in 1835 and was chairman of the selection committee when Disraeli was elected a member of the Carlton Club in 1836.[52] Chandos was also doubtless instrumental in securing Disraeli's appointment as a county magistrate, for his father was the Lord Lieutenant of Bucks.[53] In 1837 Chandos and Disraeli travelled through the night from London to Aylesbury, in order to restore Tory morale at a Bucks by-election.[54] Before the 1837 general election, Chandos helped to persuade the Tories at Maidstone to nominate Disraeli as their second candidate. In his election address, Disraeli echoed the rural politics of Chandos, declaring that he would 'on all occasions watch with vigilant solicitude over the Fortunes of the British Farmer'.[55] He was duly elected and then immediately returned to Bucks, where Chandos announced the news from the hustings at Aylesbury. Disraeli was gratified that 'those among whom I lived, and who, after all, in this world, must know me best, felt such genuine satisfaction in my success'.[56] He stayed with Chandos at Wotton and then campaigned for him in Bucks.[57]

In 1839 Chandos succeeded his father as Duke of Buckingham and soon afterwards Disraeli visited Stowe. In his 1844 novel, *Coningsby,* Disraeli described Stowe and the Duke – thinly disguised as Beaumanoir and the Duke of Agincourt. Disraeli attended the Duke's 'extremely brilliant and well arranged' assembly in London in 1843 and the 'sumptuous' celebrations at Stowe to mark the majority of his eldest son in 1845.[58] But the Duke's lavish life-style came to an abrupt end in 1847 when his gigantic debts finally caught up with him and he became a bankrupt. He was obliged to transfer all his property and debts to his son, who shut up Stowe and sold its contents at auction in 1848.[59] The Duke's bankruptcy facilitated Disraeli's election as an MP for Bucks. In 1847, Disraeli informed the Duke's heir, Chandos, that he was thinking of standing for the county:

> It is out of the question, however, that I shd. take such a step, if there be, even, a chance of your Lordship occupying a post, for which you have paramount claims, not only from your birth, but from your talents ...

Chandos's decision not to stand enabled Disraeli to press ahead with his candidature without alienating the Grenville interest. During the campaign, Disraeli denied that he was a nominee of the Grenvilles, but in 1852 the Duke of Buckingham reminded him that 'I had the gratification of first pointing out to you the road to the County'.[60] In return, Disraeli assisted the career of the Marquis of Chandos who became the third Duke of Buckingham in 1861.

Disraeli's close links with the Grenvilles have been neglected, whereas his relations with the Rothschilds have been exaggerated. Contrary to the assumptions of some historians, Disraeli had little contact with the Rothschild family in Bucks, with the exception of Anthony de Rothschild.[61] This was not surprising for Disraeli had settled in the county several decades before the Rothschilds bought their estates in the Vale of Aylesbury which was a long carriage drive from Hughenden. In any case the Rothschilds were active Liberals – Nathan was a Liberal MP for Aylesbury from 1865 to 1885 – so it would not have been politic for Disraeli to socialise too much with them.

Disraeli's close association and identification with the county of Buckinghamshire remained strong until the end of his life. At the 1874 general election, he declared that he was 'inspired by the high political spirit' of this 'sacred land'.[62] Although he retired from representing the county in 1876 he continued to take a close interest in its affairs. He was alarmed by the agricultural depression but took advantage of low land prices to add to the Hughenden estate, though he noted that 'the old tenants think me quite mad in buying land in this county'.[63] In 1879 he gave a presidential address to the Bucks Agricultural Association which entailed 'more thought and labor than if I had to bring forward a great measure in Parliament'.[64] He warned of radical attempts to destroy what he called 'the just influence of the agricultural interest'.[65]

In April 1880 Disraeli's resigned as Prime Minister after the defeat of the Conservatives at the general election. But he was consoled by the prospect of passing 'the spring and summer in the woods of Hughenden, which he had never been able to do, and longed for'.[66] But his summer at Hughenden was ruined by bad weather:

> Here we are absolutely ruined. The series of never-ending storms has destroyed all our hopes. A plentiful hay harvest drowned and the finest crops we have had for ten year laid. It is a scene of ravage; of havoc like a conquered country ... It is quite heartrending and coming from church today, my best tenants told me that they could struggle against it no longer. Wheat in Wycombe market on Friday, from New Zealand, and very fine, sold at 42s. pr. quarter – sold by samples and guaranteed to be delivered in August.[67]

At the end of the year, however, the weather turned warm and sunny and Disraeli laughed at those who trekked to the Mediterranean for winter warmth.[68] Early in 1881, the opening of Parliament obliged Disraeli to return to London, where he moved in to the first house he had ever personally owned in the city and where he died just three months later. Disraeli's will provided final proof of his personal identification with Buckinghamshire. He was to be buried, not in Westminster Abbey, but with his wife in the churchyard at Hughenden. He also left instructions that the trees at Hughenden – which he had loved so much – were not to be cut down.[69] The estate was left to his young nephew, Coningsby Disraeli, who later settled there and enlarged the house. Coningsby duly became a county magistrate, High Sheriff of Bucks, a Major in the Royal Bucks Hussars and a Tory MP – a record of which his uncle would have been proud.

After Disraeli's death, his grave at Hughenden became a place of pilgrimage for his growing army of admirers and it was decorated with wreaths from Queen Victoria and others on the anniversary of his death. On some days as many as 4,000 people visited his grave and it was estimated that over one million people came in the ten years after his death.[70] Disraeli's enthusiasm for Buckinghamshire was not an insincere political ploy, but a genuine reflection of his personal feelings, interests and connections. It originated when he moved to Bradenham with his family and fell in love with 'beechy Bucks'. His subsequent election as a knight of the shire and acquisition of Hughenden further strengthened his personal identification with the county which remained remarkably strong until his death. In a very real sense, Disraeli was a true Buckinghamshire worthy.

Roland Quinault

1   Robert Blake, *The Conservative Party from Peel to Churchill* (London, 1974), p. 130.

2   [Benjamin Disraeli], *England and France: a Cure for Ministerial Gallomania* (London, 1832), p. 13.

3   J. A. W. Gunn, John Matthews, Donald M. Schurman, M. G. Wiebe (eds.), *Benjamin Disraeli Letters Volume I: 1815–1834* (Toronto, 1982), p. 92: Benjamin Disraeli to Isaac Disraeli, 10 October 1826.

4   See: Charles Richard and Jerold M. Post, 'Disraeli's Crucial Illness', in Charles Richmond and Paul Smith (eds.), *The Self-Fashioning of Disraeli 1818-1851* (Cambridge, 1998), pp. 66–89.

5   *Disraeli Letters I*, p. 116: Disraeli to Sara Austen, 7 March 1830; p. 128: Benjamin Disraeli to Isaac Disraeli, 1 July 1830; p. 147: Benjamin Disraeli to Sarah Disraeli: 20 August 1830.

6   Benjamin Disraeli, *Endymion* (London, 1927), pp. 45–6.

7   M. G. Gunn *et al.* (eds.), *Benjamin Disraeli Letters Volume II: 1835–1837* (Toronto, 1982), p. 204: Disraeli to Pyne, 26 December 1836.

8   *Disraeli Letters II*, p. 240: Disraeli to Pyne, 5 March 1837.

9   M. G. Wiebe, J. B. Conacher, John Matthews, Mary S. Millar (eds.), *Benjamin Disraeli Letters Volume IV: 1842–1847* (Toronto, 1989), p. 259: Disraeli to Lord John Manners, 19 September 1846.

10 M. G. Wiebe *et al.* (eds.), *Benjamin Disraeli Letters Volume III: 1838–41*, (Toronto, 1987), p. 350: Disraeli to Sarah Disraeli, 24 July 1841; W. F. Monypenny and G. E. Buckle, *The Life of Benjamin Disraeli, Earl of Beaconsfield*, 2 vols. (London 1929), I. 732.

11 J. T. Coppock, 'Agricultural Changes in the Chilterns 1875–1900', *Agricultural History Review*, 9 (1961), 2–4; *Disraeli Letters II*, p. 287: Disraeli to Mrs Wyndham Lewis, 30 July 1837.

12 Paul Smith, *Disraeli, A Brief Life* (Cambridge, 1996), p. 45.

13 *Disraeli Letters III*, p. 51: Disraeli to Mrs Wyndham Lewis, 22 April 1838.

14 *Disraeli Letters I*, p. 74: Disraeli to B. Austen, 8 December 1829.

15 *Disraeli Letters II*, p. 208: Disraeli to Pyne 11 January 1837; *Disraeli Letters IV*, p. 1597 (note 3).

16 M. G. Wiebe *et al.* (eds.), *Disraeli Letters V 1848–1851* (Toronto, 1993), p. 208: Disraeli to Sarah Disraeli, 25 August 1849. See also: *Hughenden Manor* (The National Trust, 1997).

17 Helen M. Swartz and Marvin Swartz, *Disraeli's Reminiscences* (London, 1975), p. 130.

18 J. K. Fowler, *Echoes of Old Country Life* (London, 1892), p. 48.

19 Henry Lake, *Personal Reminiscences of the Rt. Hon. Benjamin Disraeli, Earl of Beaconsfield, K. G.* (London, n.d.), p. 36.

20 John Vincent (ed.), *Disraeli, Derby and the Conservative Party: Journals and Memoirs of Edward Henry Lord Stanley 1849–1869* (Hassocks, 1978), pp. 346–7: diary entries for 23, 24 December 1869.

21 *The Times*, 27 September 1871.

22 See, for example, *Disraeli Letters II*, p. 660: Disraeli to Mrs Wyndham Lewis, 1 September 1837.

23 *The Times*, 24 October 1836.

24 *Disraeli Letters II*, p. 673: Disraeli to Sarah Disraeli, 16 November 1837.

25 *Parliamentatry Debates*, third series, 83 (1846), c. 1340.

26 Monypenny and Buckle, *Disraeli*, I. 1287: Disraeli to Mrs Brydges Willyams, 14 October 1862.

27 M. G. Wiebe, Mary S. Millar, Ann P. Robson (eds.), *Benjamin Disraeli Letters Volume VI: 1852–1856* (Toronto, 1997), p. 506: Disraeli to Sarah Brydges Willyams, 6 November 1856.

28 Swartz, *Disraeli's Reminscences*, p. 148.

29 Fowler, *Echoes of Old Country Life*, p. 43.

30 *Disraeli Letters II*, p. 196: Disraeli to Pyne, 5 December 1836.

31 Lake, *Reminiscences of Disraeli*, p. 1.

32 Monypenny and Buckle, *Disraeli*, I. 840–41: Disraeli's speech at Newport Pagnell, 9 June 1847.

33 *Parliamentary Debates*, third series, 103 (1849), c. 452.

34 Lake, *Reminiscences of Disraeli*, p. 20, speech at Buckingham, 12 June 1847.

35 Monypenny and Buckle, *Disraeli*, I. 1044–45: Disraeli to Lord Stanley, 9 November 1849.

36 Ibid., I. 1127–28: Disraeli to Sarah Disraeli, 17 October 1851.

37 Ibid., I. 622–23: Disraeli to Lady Bradford, 6 February 1874.

38 Disraeli, *Endymion*, p. 362.

39 Blake, *Conservative Party*, pp. 85–6: William Joliffe to Derby, 23 October 1855 [Derby Papers 158/10].

40 Smith, *Disraeli*, p. 111; Davis, *Disraeli*, p. 94.
41 Monypenny and Buckle, *Disraeli*, I. 1573–4: Disraeli to Lord Stanley, 9 August 1858.
42 Bodleian Library, Oxford, Dep. Hughenden 29/1, fol. 29: T. Tyrwhitt Drake to Disraeli, 26 May 1847.
43 Dep.Hughenden 29/1, fol. 68: Sir H. Verney to Disraeli, 5 June 1847.
44 Swartz, *Disraeli's Reminiscences*, p. 132.
45 *Disraeli Letters III*, p. 149: Disraeli to Sarah Disraeli, 25? February 1839.
46 *Disraeli Letters IV*, pp. 162–63: Disraeli to Lord Carrington, 15 April 1845.
47 John Beckett, *The Rise and Fall of the Grenvilles, Dukes of Buckingham and Chandos, 1710–1921* (Manchester, 1994), p. 255.
48 *Disraeli Letters I*, p. 286 note 2.
49 Ibid., p. 289: the endorsement to a letter from Disraeli to Henry Gwillim, 22 June 1832.
50 Ibid., p. 323: Disraeli to Sarah Disraeli, 14 February 1833.
51 Ibid., Appendix II, p. 444: Disraeli's aide-memoire, November 1834.
52 *Disraeli Letters II*, p. 31: Disraeli to Sarah Disraeli, 26? April 1835.
53 Henry Reeve (ed.), *The Greville Memoirs*, 8 vols. (London, 1889), V. 68: entry for 15 December 1841.
54 *Disraeli Letters II*, p. 234: Disraeli to William Pyne, 16 February 1837.
55 Ibid., p. 276: Disraeli to the Freemen and Electors of Maidstone, 1 July 1837.
56 Ibid., p. 287: Disraeli to Mrs Wyndham Lewis, 30 July 1837.
57 Ibid., p. 308: Disraeli to Mrs Wyndham Lewis, 29 October 1837.
58 *Disraeli Letters IV*, p. 99: Disraeli to Sarah Disraeli, 19 June 1843; p. 154: Disraeli to Sarah Disraeli, 20 January 1845.
59 *The Times*, 14 August 1848.
60 Dep. Hughenden 120/1, fols. 97–9: Duke of Buckingham to Disraeli, March 1852.
61 Stanley Weintraub, *Disraeli, A Biography* (London, 1993), p. 396.
62 *The Times*, 11 February 1874.
63 Monypenny and Buckle, *Disraeli*, II. 1348.
64 The Marquis of Zetland (ed.), *The Letters of Disraeli to Ladies Bradford and Chesterfield*, 2 vols., (London, 1929), II. 237: Disraeli to Lady Bradford, 2 September 1879.
65 Monypenny and Buckle, *Disraeli*, II. 1371: Disraeli's speech at Aylesbury, 18 September 1879.
66 Ibid., II. 1396: Memorandum by Lord Barrington, 4 April 1880.
67 Ibid., II. 1456–7: Disraeli to Lady Bradford, 18 July 1880.
68 Ibid., II. 1465: Disraeli to Lady Chesterfield, 7 December 1880.
69 Lake, *Reminiscences of Disraeli*, p. 101.
70 Ibid., p. 104.

Fig. 5 **Mary Anne, Viscountess Beaconsfield** by J.G. Middleton
Oil on canvas, 114.3 x 88.9 cm; reproduced by permission of Hughenden Manor (The National Trust).

Disraeli and Women

'Mr DISRAELI has had to make his position,' Lord Derby told Queen Victoria in 1851, 'and men who make their positions will say and do things which are not necessary to be said or done by those for whom positions are provided.' Derby was explaining Disraeli's bad behaviour towards Peel over the Corn Laws, but his remark contains a wider truth. Unlike Derby and most of his colleagues, Disraeli was not a member of the Victorian governing class. Nor was he a meritocrat, the gilded product of the University of Oxford or Cambridge: unlike Peel or Gladstone he didn't glide into Parliament on the strength of a double first. Born in a library (his father's) and educated at home, he was a self-made adventurer, a Jew and an outsider; a failed lawyer, a dandy and a novelist who was deeply in debt. Like many outsiders, he owed much of his success to the influence of women.

The first woman to advance Disraeli's career was Mrs Sara Austen. The wife of a family solicitor, she was eight years older than Disraeli, and she played a critical role in assisting publication of the manuscript that eventually became *Vivian Grey* (1826). The novel was inspired by the fiasco of the *Representative* newspaper, when the publisher John Murray pulled the plug on the twenty-one year old Disraeli's wildly impractical scheme to outdo *The Times*. *Vivian Grey*, which was published anonymously, created a *succes de scandale*. When Disraeli's authorship was revealed, Sara Austen supported him in his disgrace. 'Ben' plunged into depression and inertia, and Sara Austen and her husband travelled with him to Italy. Disraeli, who was already in debt, borrowed shamelessly from the husband while flirting with the wife. He collaborated again with Sara Austen over the sequel to *Vivian Grey*, but by now he had tired of her, and he turned to other married women, such as Clara Bolton, the wife of his doctor.

Until his marriage, the most important woman in Disraeli's life was his older sister Sarah. She was unmarried, a fact for which Disraeli partly blamed himself, as her fiancé, William Meredith, died of smallpox while on the Grand Tour with Disraeli in 1831. Meredith's death brought Benjamin and Sarah close together. In *Alroy* (1833), the novel he wrote about a thirteenth-century Jewish prince who rebels against the Persian caliphate, Disraeli celebrated the love between Alroy/Disraeli and his sister Miriam. 'I know not love,' says Alroy, 'save that pure affection which doth subsist between me and … my sister.' Back in London after his Grand Tour, Disraeli tracked his career as a dandy on the make in diary letters to Sarah which, in spite (or perhaps because of) a strong element of make believe, still leap off the page today. She was his confidante. His conquests, repartee, gossip – all were gleefully related to 'My dear Sa'.

'Ah, poor Sa!' remarked Disraeli on her death in 1859, 'we've lost our audience.' But Sarah was more than that. Dutifully caring for her aging parents at Bradenham, the manor house they rented in Bucks, Sarah lived vicariously through her adored brother Ben. Brother-sister relationships that combined companionship with shared creativity were a Romantic trope, glamorised by Byron, the hero of Disraeli's youth. Disraeli and Sarah wrote a novel together, *Hartlebury*, which ends abruptly when the Disraeli figure is murdered (Sarah wrote this part of the book).

Sarah provided emotional support and unconditional love of the kind that Disraeli seems never to have received from his mother. Maria Disraeli is a silent figure, a non-writer in a literary family, but the fragments of evidence that survive suggest that she showed her talented son little affection. She never gave him the approval that he craved. After his parents died, Disraeli wrote a memoir of his father which, to Sarah's dismay, contained no reference to 'our dear Mother' – it was almost as if he were blotting her out. The central figure in his childhood was his father, the antiquarian and man of letters Isaac D'Israeli.

Psycho-historians have speculated that Disraeli's failed relationship with his mother was key to his political drive. He has been labelled a 'narcissistic character' who, deprived of maternal affection and support, had a constant need to compensate for that lack. He hungered for attention and approval to counteract his inner sense of worthlessness. He was drawn towards older women, who played the role of mother figures.[1]

Disraeli's early novels, from *Vivian Grey* through *The Young Duke* and *Alroy* to *Contarini Fleming*, contain few memorable portraits of women. They are not romantic novels, but *Bildungsromans* – accounts of a young man's formative journey through life. They are all more or less autobiographical. *Alroy* explores a central element of Disraeli's persona, his Jewishness. *The Young Duke*, which Disraeli later disowned as a potboiler, is a silver-fork novel which is held together by a narrator whose voice is Disraeli's own. *Contarini Fleming* is the most overtly autobiographical of Disraeli's novels: the thinly masked story of his life. It contains a vivid account of the nervous collapse that he suffered in 1830, before his Grand Tour to the Middle East. Letters home and travel diaries are reproduced verbatim. The central character in all of these early novels is Disraeli himself. He used his fiction to try on new roles for size, reinventing himself as a Romantic hero in *Contarini Fleming*, a Jewish prince (*Alroy*), a political impresario (*Vivian Grey*) or a jaunty, cynical Don Juan in *The Young Duke*.

The first love story that Disraeli wrote was *Henrietta Temple* (1837), which is a fictionalized account of his affair with Henrietta Sykes. She was the wife of Sir Francis Sykes, the dissolute heir to an Indian fortune who lived at Basildon. This slightly squalid adulterous affair with a woman who teetered on the brink of the demi-monde was idealised by Disraeli into a grand passion. His letters to Henrietta have disappeared, but Henrietta's to him, which survive among the Disraeli Papers, show her signing herself, significantly, 'Your mother'. Never one to waste valuable copy, Disraeli reproduced many of Henrietta's letters word for word in his novel.

Disraeli's relationship with Henrietta Sykes was scandalous, even by the standards of the 1830s. Disraeli shamelessly used Henrietta to further his political ambitions. Having stood unsuccessfully at High Wycombe as a Radical and then as an Independent, he realized that his

Fig. 6 **Henrietta Sykes** by Daniel Maclise, R.A., 1837
Detail of original watercolour, 113 x 65 cm. On loan from Sir John Sykes, Bt. Reproduced with permission of Sir John Sykes.

only chance of entering politics depended on attaching himself to an influential patron. Henrietta spotted a suitable candidate in Lord Lyndhurst, the recently widowed Tory lawyer, whom she cultivated for Disraeli's sake. Lyndhurst was notoriously susceptible to women, and soon Henrietta was sharing her bed with him as well as Disraeli. Henrietta's lovemaking did the trick: Disraeli gained work as Lyndhurst's political assistant, which gave him access to Tory circles. Henrietta, however, was insatiable. She began an affair with the painter Daniel Maclise who was painting her portrait – he was a friend of Disraeli, whom he had drawn at least twice. After a stormy row, Disraeli broke off the relationship.

Disraeli's marriage to Mary Anne Wyndham Lewis in 1839 was a characteristic mixture of cynicism and romanticism. She was twelve years older than him, the wealthy widow of Wyndham Lewis, who had been Disraeli's fellow member for Maidstone, the seat he won in 1837. Though she turned out to be less wealthy than he expected, she provided the financial security that Disraeli desperately needed, as well as a fashionable address on Park Lane at 1, Grosvenor Gate.

It is no coincidence that Disraeli only began to make a mark in politics after his marriage. Not only did Mary Anne pay his debts, buying off the creditors who lurked like sharks, always threatening to expose him and destroy his political career, but she was also a mother figure who provided an emotional anchor for the mercurial Disraeli. Though uneducated (according to Disraeli, she could never remember which came first, the Greeks or the Romans), she had sound practical common sense, which was something Disraeli conspicuously lacked.

He was genuinely devoted to her. Thin and scrawny, mutton dressed as lamb and prone to embarrassing remarks, Mary Anne was a figure of ridicule. To his credit, Disraeli was loyal. 'Why my dear, you are more like a mistress than a wife,' he famously remarked when the 75-year old Mary Anne stayed up late with a bottle of champagne and a Fortnum & Mason's pie to welcome him back from his victory over the 1867 Reform Act. Disraeli's loyalty to his wife was the only thing about him that Gladstone found he could whole-heartedly praise in the obituary speech he was obliged to make after his rival's death. (The effort gave him diarrhoea.)

As for Mary Anne, her devotion was unquestioned. She cut his hair and treasured every lock. She squirreled away every letter he ever wrote. Once her hand was caught in the door of her carriage on the way to Parliament, where Disraeli was due to make an important speech. In spite of the pain, which was considerable, she never said a word.

Disraeli had few male friends of his own generation, preferring to form friendships with younger men. As Robert Blake wrote, 'To say that Disraeli only gave his confidence to young men and old women would perhaps be an overstatement, but not an outrageous one.'[2] The Young England movement of the 1840s depended for its impact on Disraeli's ability to act as impresario to a group of young aristocratic Tories. Disraeli was closest to George Smythe, intelligent but wayward, whom he idealised as the eponymous hero of his novel *Coningsby*. Later, in the 1850s, Disraeli gave his confidence to the young, fashionable and (according to Blake) 'feather-headed' Lord Henry Lennox, who was his private secretary. Lennox, a younger son of the Duke of Richmond, was perpetually searching for a wealthy heiress, but remained a lifelong bachelor. Blake suggests that Disraeli's effusively affectionate letters ('I can only tell you that I love you,' he told Smythe in September 1852) should be discounted as the hyperbole of the time; not all biographers would agree.

Older women continued to engage him. One of oddest episodes in Disraeli's career is his friendship with Mrs Brydges Willyams. She was a wealthy widow of well over eighty when she first met Disraeli in the 1851 or 1853, and she shared Disraeli's Jewish ancestry – in fact she believed herself (probably wrongly) to be connected to him. Enticed no doubt by her promise to leave him money in her will, Disraeli paid her visits in Torquay, and, after Sarah Disraeli's death, Mrs

Brydges Willyams became his female confidante, the recipient of hundreds of his sparkling, gossipy letters. When she died in 1865, she left Disraeli well over £30,000, on condition that he was buried next to her in Hughenden Parish Church. Dizzy, Mary Anne and Mrs Brydges Willyams share a grave outside the church today.

As Prime Minister, Disraeli was famously successful in forming a rapport with Queen Victoria. As ever with Dizzy, political opportunism combined with a touch of romanticism. The mourning Victoria was a Tory in politics, and sympathized politically with Disraeli more than she did Gladstone. Disraeli saw the political capital to be made from this. He played a key role in persuading the grieving monarch to emerge from mourning – even if the price was giving way to her on such political issues as the Royal Titles Bill of 1876, which made her Empress of India. Disraeli laid on the flattery with a trowel. 'We authors ma'm,' he famously remarked, and in his letters he showered the Faery Queen with compliments, which were often as absurd as they were extravagant.

Mary Anne Disraeli died in 1872, Disraeli having persuaded the Queen to make her Viscountess Beaconsfield in her own right in 1868. Gouty, wheezing and alone, Disraeli craved female company. 'I live for power and the affections,' he declared, and embarked on an epistolary romance with two elderly sisters, Lady Bradford and Lady Chesterfield. Anne Chesterfield was a widow of 70 when Disraeli began to write to her; he proposed to her because she was available, in order to be near her younger sister, Selina Bradford, who was not, but whom he preferred. Lady Chesterfield sensibly refused him, but Disraeli maintained an animated flirtatious correspondence with the two sisters throughout the 1874-80 Government which gave him great emotional support.

Jane Ridley

[1] See Charles Richmond and Jerold M. Post, 'Disraeli's Crucial Illness', in Charles Richmond and Paul Smith (eds.), *The Self-Fashioning of Disraeli* (Cambridge, 1998).
[2] Robert Blake, *Disraeli* (London, 1966), p. 326.

The Catalogue

CHAPTER ONE

1804–25

Bookish Beginnings: 'I was born in a library'

THE FACTS of Benjamin Disraeli's birth are clear-cut. He was born on 21 December 1804 in his parents' house, No. 6 Bedford Row (afterwards 22 Theobald's Road), close to Grays Inn, in central London (today's WC1 area). He was the second of the five children of Isaac D'Israeli (1766–1848) and his wife Maria (d. 1847), a member of the Basevi family which produced the first Jewish-born barrister practising in England and the architect of the Fitzwilliam Museum in Cambridge. Isaac was a literary figure, the author of the well-regarded *Curiosities of Literature* and other works. Through friendship with his publisher, the legendary John Murray, Isaac D'Israeli was involved in establishing the *Quarterly Review* in 1809, knew both Sir Walter Scott and Lord Byron, and was one of the guests when the two great writers famously met at Murray's house, 50 Albemarle Street, in 1815. It was into this literary, imaginative world that Disraeli was born and nurtured.

Unlike many of his future colleagues Disraeli attended neither public school (possibly for financial reasons he was sent to boarding schools) nor university, but rounded off his formal education at home and then trained for a career in the law. Introduced to the profession through Maples, a friend of his father, Disraeli was temperamentally unsuited to be either a solicitor or barrister and abandoned the law in 1831. His early experiences and socialization reinforced a disposition to intellectualize life.

His family life was crucial in shaping his personality, not least a sequence of events in 1817 when he was nearly 13. Following a quarrel with his late father's synagogue over subscriptions Isaac D'Israeli abandoned the Jewish faith to which he was only loosely attached. The move had profound consequences for Disraeli. The adolescent Disraeli was separated from a distinctive aspect of his identity at a key stage in his development and, on the advice of one of Isaac's friends, baptised into the Church of England. If Disraeli had remained a member of the Jewish faith he would never have become Prime Minister, as practising Jews were excluded from Parliament until 1858, by which time Disraeli would have been too old to embark on a political career.

But this loss of part of his nascent self and the need to be reunited with it fed into his quest for the aristocratic Jewish past he craved and fictionalized in his novels, and for the intellectual arguments which would validate his personification of a Jewish past and Christian present in contemporary society. In 1822 Disraeli altered his surname, removing the apostrophe – a distinction which many of his correspondents ignored well into his middle years.

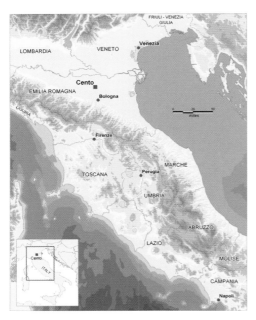

I

Italian Sephardic origins[1]

10.5 x 6.25 cm
Collins Bartholomew Ltd. 2003

Digital map created by Nigel James of the Map
Section, Bodleian Library, showing the location of
Cento, from where Disraeli's paternal grandfather
had emigrated. Cento lies some 100 miles east of
Venice – the city adopted by Disraeli as his
ancestral base. His Basevi grandfather had
emigrated from Verona.

2-3

Isaac and Maria D'Israeli

Isaac D'Israeli (1766–1848)
by Daniel Maclise, RA, July 1828
Pencil and wash on paper, c. 25 x 29 cm, reproduced by permission of Hughenden Manor (The
National Trust).

As parents Isaac and Maria had very different
attitudes towards their eldest son. Isaac, author of
an essay on literary genius, fostered notions of
intellectual brilliance but, as Disraeli would later
confide to his secretary Montagu Corry, he did
not understand his son.

4
'My dearest Sa'
Sarah D'Israeli (d. 1859) by Daniel Maclise, RA,
May 1828
Pencil drawing on paper, c. 33 x 35.5 cm, reproduced by permission of Hughenden Manor (The National Trust).

The close relationship between Disraeli and Sarah was fictionalized in his novel *Alroy* (1833). Under the pseudonyms Cherry and Fair Star they co-wrote *A year at Hartlebury* (1834), a political novel inspired by Disraeli's candidacy in the 1832 Wycombe election. Perhaps inevitably the closeness did not survive Disraeli's marriage. Disraeli had two other surviving siblings: Ralph (1809–98), who inherited Hughenden, and James (1813–68).

Maria D'Israeli (d. 1847)
by Daniel Maclise, RA, June 1828
Pencil drawing, c. 25 x 29 cm, reproduced by permission of Hughenden Manor (The National Trust).

Disraeli's relations with his mother were problematic. Depicting her as the stepmother in his novel, *Contarini Fleming* (1832), conveys the emotional distance between the two; a striving for maternal affection and approval coloured his adult relationships. Isaac cast his son in a heroic light but Maria's assessment of her elder son's abilities was more pragmatic.

5
Man of Letters

Reproduced by permission of Hughenden Manor
(The National Trust).

The five-volume anthology, *Curiosities of
Literature* (1791–1834), now in the Library at
Hughenden, is probably Isaac's best known work.
His other main publication was the five-volume
Commentaries on the life and reign of Charles I
(1828–30), a topic well-suited to his romantic
conservatism. For this study he was awarded a
DCL by the University of Oxford in 1832. In
addition to these major works Isaac was also the
author of several now-forgotten novels and
poems.

7

Home

(2003)

6 Bloomsbury Square, London home of Isaac D'Israeli and his family from 1817. The house, dating from the mid-eighteenth century, is conveniently close to the British Museum which then housed the future British Library's collections.

6

Home from home

31.8 x 40 cm

John Murray Archive

Imaginary recreation c.1850 by L. Werner (1824–1901) of the meeting in John Murray's drawing room, 50 Albermarle Street, London, Spring 1815. Left to right: Isaac D'Israeli, John Murray II, Sir John Barrow, George Canning, J. W. Croker, Sir Walter Scott and Lord Byron.

8

Disraeli the trainee lawyer

32 x 30 cm

Dep. Hughenden 10, fol. 13

Copy of indenture at Messrs Swain, Stevens, Maples, Pearce & Hunt, solicitors, 10 November 1821. The experience gained in business affairs proved to be a mixed blessing when combined with his precociousness; unwise speculations saddled him with debt for much of his adult life.

yours affectionately
John Murray

BORN 1778 — DIED 1843.

From the Portrait by Pickersgill, R.A.

9

John Murray, Publisher and family friend

John Murray II (1778–1843), Engraving by
Pickersgill, RA

32 x 25 cm

John Murray Archive

John Murray was a doyen of publishing in the first
half of the nineteenth century. Murray was
Byron's publisher and literary executor; his 'list'
included Jane Austen and George Borrow and
many other leading writers.

10

Young Disraeli in Albemarle Street

23 x 37.5 cm

Dep. Hughenden 8/1, fols. 4^v–5^r

This letter written on 4 August 1825 from Disraeli
to his father describes an evening at a party in
Albemarle Street hosted by John Murray for
former and current African expeditions. Friendship with Murray would further Disraeli's bookish
tendencies and literary talent but founder over
their disastrous financial collaboration.

CHAPTER TWO

1824–31

Adventures at Home and Abroad

DISRAELI'S TWENTIES were a period of exploration, shaping his ideas and sense of self. He was very much a young man in a hurry, seeking fame and wealth to fulfil his sense of destiny. As a writer and novelist raiding history and his own life for copy he achieved the first – though at times it was closer to notoriety; the second eluded him: he was no financial *wunderkind*. Part of the notoriety was due to his flamboyant appearance. Disraeli wore the bright colours, tight trousers, frilled shirts and large jewels of a dandy – a foppish, feminized style personified and led by Count D'Orsay (1801–52), a member of the Byron circle and future mentor to Disraeli.

Byron's life was a great inspiration to Disraeli as for many others. For Disraeli it percolated into his travels through Europe and the Middle East in the mid-1820s and early 1830s, and into his writing and friendships, and even extended to finding employment in his father's household for Byron's former gondolier and manservant Battista Flacieri (Tita), whom he had encountered in Malta in the summer of 1830. Byron died in Tita's arms at Missolonghi, as Isaac D'Israeli would years later at Bradenham, the D'Israeli family home in Buckinghamshire.

During these formative years the emotional patterns in Disraeli's life emerge: close relationships with older women (often Sarah D'Israeli look-alikes) and younger men; periods of frenetic activity and creativity followed by nervous exhaustion and collapse, relieved by periods of solitude in the country.

II

Tasting Europe

16.5 x 19 cm

Dep. Hughenden 11/1/3, pp. 26–7

Concerned by his son's health Isaac took Disraeli on his first trip abroad, a six-week tour of Belgium and the Rhine in the summer of 1824, accompanied by William Meredith, Sarah's (then) unofficial fiancé. The early part of the journey from London to Aix is recorded here. Most of the entries are in pencil and too faint to read with ease, but this description of an attempt to visit

Rubens' house in Antwerp on 2 August 1824 gives some indication of Disraeli's enthusiasm for architecture – especially churches – paintings, food and landscape, and of his observations on history and local custom. Disraeli didn't keep a diary on the journey's second leg but he did decide to become a writer – and he drew on his experiences in his first novel, *Vivian Grey*.

12

Grand Designs: John Murray and *The Representative*

26.7 x 41.1 cm
Reproduced by permission of the John Murray
Archive.

The 1820s were a period of frenzied speculation.
Investing in Mexican mining companies was one of
the get-rich-quick schemes – a nineteenth-century
dotcom boom. Disraeli, barely 20 years old and
working as John Murray's assistant, became part of
a mining shares partnership and involved the
publisher in the scheme and in publishing
promotional pamphlets. By 1825 the enterprise had
a £7,000 deficit. Disraeli's exact share of the losses
is unclear but the financial consequences haunted
him for years.[2] Undeterred by these events he
encouraged Murray to realize the latter's
longstanding ambition to launch a daily newspaper.

This volume includes letters with coded passages
describing Disraeli's discussions in Edinburgh with
Sir Walter Scott (1771–1832) and his son-in-law
J. G. Lockhart, who was invited to join the
enterprise. In letter No. 11, September 1825, Disraeli
naively records their surprise that Murray has sent
the young Disraeli and his belief that Scott and
Lockhart are in 'perfect & complete compatibility'
with him. When gripped by an idea Disraeli could
find himself impaled on reality. Back in London
Disraeli recruited the *Representative's* correspondents but the scheme ended in disaster partly
through Murray placing too much faith in
Disraeli's abilities, a factor Disraeli later recognized.
In the failed enterprise Murray lost £26,000.

13–14
Vivian Grey
19 x 23 cm
Vol. 1 of 2 volumes, 1ˢᵗ edition (London, 1826),
8° L 138,
pp. 52–3.

Partly inspired by Plumer Ward's *Tremaine* (from whom the D'Israeli family rented a house and to whom Disraeli dedicated *Popanilla*) Disraeli's 'silver fork' novel revolves around the adventures of Grey, Disraeli's fictionalized self. Brittle in tone the novel is also prophetic – pointing towards Disraeli's decision to enter politics, the conflict with Peel in the 1840s and, through its publisher Colburn – a client of Austen and a substitute for Murray, his link with Longmans.[3] (See Annabel Jones, 'Fame and Reputation: a Novelist and his Publisher', pp. 21–28.) It earned the near-bankrupt Disraeli £500, £140 of which he sent to Murray in payment of a co-investor's debt. Fictionalizing the *Representative* saga and depicting Murray as the inebriate Marquess of Carabas would lead to Murray severing connections with the D'Israelis, much to the family's chagrin.

This extract is full of telling comment about the ambitious young Disraeli/*Grey*; the grand object so much desired – to be in the Senate – is revealed on p. 54. Gladstone, Disraeli's future Liberal rival, referred disparagingly in his diary to the novel being clever but trashy. Part two, Volumes 3–5, appeared in 1827 to less acclaim. Twenty-five years later Disraeli, embarrassed by the image projected in the novel, tried to exclude it from the 1853 edition of his collected works.

52   VIVIAN GREY.

and conversationised with any stray four year older not yet sent to bed.

But Vivian Grey was an elegant, lively lad, with just enough of dandyism to preserve him from committing *gaucheries*, and with a devil of a tongue. All men, I am sure, will agree with me when I say, that the only rival to be feared by a man of spirit is—a clever boy.— What makes them so popular with the women, it is not for me to explain ; however, Lady Julia Knighton, and Mrs. Frank Delmington, and half a score of dames of fashion, (and some of them very pretty !) were always patronizing our hero, who really found an evening spent in their company not altogether dull ; for there is no fascination so irresistible to a boy, as the smile of a married woman. Vivian had really passed such a recluse life for the last two years and a half, that he had quite forgotten that he was once considered a very fascinating fellow ; and so, determined to discover what right he

VIVIAN GREY.   53

ever had to such a reputation, master Vivian entered into all those amourettes in very beautiful style.

But Vivian Grey was a young and tender plant in a moral hot-house. His character was developing itself too soon. Although his evenings were now generally passed in the manner we have alluded to, this boy was, during the rest of the day, a hard and indefatigable student ; and having now got through an immense series of historical reading, he had stumbled upon a branch of study certainly the most delightful in the world,—but, for a boy, as certainly the most pernicious,—THE STUDY OF POLITICS.

And now every thing was solved ! the inexplicable longings of his soul, which had so often perplexed him, were at length explained. The *want*, the indefinable *want*, which he had so constantly experienced, was at last supplied ; the grand object on which to bring the

15
Rave reviews
18.5 x 23 cm
Dep. Hughenden 12/2, fols. 18–19

Disraeli's debut as a novelist was spectacular. Volume 1 of *Vivian Grey* was published anonymously in April 1826. To maximize impact the draft was copied out by Sara Austen to conceal its authorship. Sara, considerably older than Disraeli, was married to his neighbour the lawyer Benjamin Austen, for whom Disraeli had worked. Both Austens were his patrons, she emotionally, he financially. Here she refers to the *Star*

reviewer's comparisons with similar novels like *Mathilda* and *Tremaine*, set in 'fashionable' aristocratic society and aimed at middle class readers; the author was a 'lively and accomplished writer' and his 'ingenuity' praised. By July the enthusiasm among high society and reviewers turned to scorn when it was discovered that the satire had been written by a youthful onlooker, not an insider.

16

Author & dandy

'The Author of Vivian Grey' by Daniel Maclise,
RA.
Original drawing on paper, 29.2 x 21.8 cm,
reproduced by permission of Hughenden Manor
(The National Trust).

The Irish-born Maclise (1806–70) also produced
fine portraits of Isaac and Sarah Disraeli. Later
his affair with Disraeli's then mistress would
rebound disastrously on his friend.

17

Refuge at Bradenham

'Bradenham Manor from S. E. 1850'
Original watercolour, 30 x 83.8 cm, reproduced by
permission of Hughenden Manor (The National
Trust).

After the publication of the first part of *Vivian
Grey* Disraeli's health buckled under the strain of
his frenetic life style, failures and mounting debts.
Travelling to Italy with the Austens between
August and October brought some respite but
most of 1827 was lost to illness and depression,
though he managed to complete the second part of
his novel and register as a pupil barrister. *Popanilla*
appeared in 1828 but the only really positive
development during this dark phase was the
D'Israeli family settling permanently in
Buckinghamshire, at Bradenham Manor, leaving
London because of Mrs D'Israeli's poor health. It
was to Bradenham that Disraeli retreated in
December 1829. The sixteenth-century house,
remodelled in the eighteenth, is now National
Trust offices.

In the spring of 1830 Disraeli's health had
improved sufficiently for him to work on two
books, *The Young Duke* and *Alroy*, and to resume
his raffish social life. It was now that he became
close friends with the writer and future Colonial
Secretary Edward Bulwer Lytton, later Lord
Lytton (1803–73). He also became involved with
Clara Bolton at this time, his own doctor's wife,
but he was far from fully restored and there were
worrying reminders of Isaac's own breakdown at
around this age. Travelling was again the antidote
– as well as an escape from pressing creditors (his
debts amounted to £4,500). The consequences of
his visit with Meredith to Spain and the Middle
East (funded by money for *The Young Duke* and
the Austen advance) would reach far beyond his
return in October 1831, for they were crucial in
shaping Disraeli's perceptions of himself, his racial
origins and the wider world.

lithe and clear tho' sallow – but you have seen I Mercandotti. As she advances, if she do not lose her shape, she resembles Juno rather than Venus. Majestic she ever is, and if her feet are less twinkling than in her first career, look on her hand and you'll forgive them all.

There is a calm voluptuousness about the life here that wonderfully accords with my disposition so that if I were resident and had my intellect at command, I do not know any place where I could make it more productive. The imagination is ever at work, and beauty and grace are not scared away by those sounds and sights, those constant cares, and changing feelings which are the proud possession of our free land of eastern winds.

18

Ancestral Voices

Extract from Letter 94, reproduced from *Benjamin Disraeli Letters, Volume 1: 1815–1834* (Toronto, 1982) pp. 140–1.

Disraeli's relations with his mother are often described as difficult but the surviving letters suggest that it improved with distance. Here, in an extract from a letter written from Granada in August 1830, he writes at length about Spanish women: 'There is a calm voluptuousness about the life here that wonderfully accords with my disposition so that if I were resident and had my intellect at command, I do not know any place where I could make it more productive'. By

contrast, he describes 'the sounds and sights, those constant cares and changing feelings…' of England. Some indication of his growing identification with Spain would weave itself into a fantastical recreation of his paternal family's origins. They were cast as aristocratic Jews driven out in the great exodus and finally coming to rest in Venice (here there is a modicum of truth but the location is more ghetto than palazzo).

19
Living the legend
25.5 x 42.5 cm
Dep. Hughenden 5/1, fols. 2–3

From Spain Meredith and Disraeli progressed to
Malta. Here they met their mutual (and then
disreputable) friend James Clay (d. 1873) whose
support as a Radical MP for the 1867 Reform Bill
would later be crucial to Disraeli, and Tita,
Byron's former servant now in his employ. They
continued on to Greece, Turkey, Cyprus, the Holy
Land and Egypt. Disraeli's imagination, his
sexuality and sensuality were given full rein.
Orientalism attracted him. He identified with the
Grand Vizier's cause against the 'rebels' in Albania
(whereas Byron had opposed the Turks in
Greece), donned Turkish clothes and lived à la
Turque. He rhapsodized over Constantinople
(visited by Byron 1810–11) and the Holy Land.
Meredith left his companions in December to
travel alone, their reunion in Egypt ending
tragically when Meredith died from smallpox in
July. In this letter Disraeli writes to Sarah
describing Meredith's death and, characteristically,
re-directs any spare affection towards himself 'If I
cannot be to you all of our lost friend, at least we
will feel, that Life can never be a blank while
illumined by the pure & perfect love of a Sister &
a Brother'.

20
'Tita'
Giovanni Falcieri (1798–1874), by Daniel Maclise,
RA 1836, signed.
Original chalk on paper, 69 x 55.8 cm; bought by
Disraeli in 1870, reproduced by permission of
Hughenden Manor (The National Trust).

Disraeli's commitment to Byron's memory
extended to his recommendation to Queen
Victoria that Tita's widow, whom Tita had met
while working in the Bradenham household,
should be awarded a pension on the strength of
Tita's service to Byron. Tita served as house
steward to Isaac for 16 years.

Gallery of Affection, Friendship and Association, 1820s–1830s

Most of the photographs in the four 'galleries' in this book (see pp. 93–96, 111–117) are taken from portraits hanging at Hughenden, including several from the 'Gallery of Affection' which now hang on the staircase.

21

George Gordon Byron, 6ᵗʰ Baron Byron
(1788–1824), by R. Westhall, RA, 1813
Oil on canvas, 124.5 x 104.1 cm, reproduced by permission of Hughenden Manor (The National Trust).

22

John Singleton Copley, 1ˢᵗ Baron Lyndhurst
(1772–1863) standing in the House of Lords, by Count D'Orsay, assisted by Landseer, n.d.
Oil on canvas, 127 x 66 cm, reproduced by permission of Hughenden Manor (The National Trust). Originally owned by Gladstone, who sold it in 1875. It was bought for and presented to Disraeli by a group of Conservative MPs.

23
James Clay M.P. (d. 1873), by A. S. Wortley
Oil on canvas, 76.2 x 81.3 cm, reproduced by
permission of Hughenden Manor (The National
Trust).

24
Daniel O'Connell (1775–1847) leader of the
Irish MPs, from a miniature by T. Carrick
Engraving, 25 x 17 cm, in Thomas Archer,
William Ewart Gladstone and his Contemporaries
(London, 1883).
2288 d.1

26
Edward Bulwer Lytton, 1ˢᵗ Baron Lytton
(1803–73), after Maclise, n.d.
Oil on canvas, 127 x 83.8 cm, reproduced by
permission of Hughenden Manor (The National
Trust).

25
Alfred, Count D'Orsay (1801–52), by John
Wood, RA, 1841
Oil on canvas, 111.8 x 81.3 cm, reproduced by
permission of Hughenden Manor (The National
Trust). The painting was purchased by Disraeli
from D'Orsay's widow.

CHAPTER THREE

1832–7

New Horizons

DURING THE five years between his return to England and his election to Parliament Disraeli continued to explore his personality, using the literary, historical and political dimensions of his imagination and his driving ambition to connect with a Britain in transition. Industrialization, urbanization and the extension of the franchise, three of the main engines for change, would radically alter British society and present Disraeli's generation of political leaders with challenging agenda. Disraeli would emerge as one of the key figures shaping Victorian Britain in the second and third quarters of the century. But in his thirties he was a prolific writer of articles, books and pamphlets, standing for Parliament five times, falling in love – and dodging his creditors.

27
En Voyage
23 x 37.5 cm
Dep. Hughenden 12/2, fols. 154–5

Disraeli announced to his father his intention of standing for Parliament in this letter written on board HMS *Hermes* in October 1831 in which (overleaf) he expresses concern that Isaac may not have received his earlier one announcing Meredith's death. Here he notes that his fellow passenger, Henry Stanley, had received a letter in Cadiz that the bill to extend the franchise would be lost – an outcome they could 'barely credit'. When this younger son of the 13th Earl of Derby went missing on arrival in London some of the Stanley family suspected Disraeli of introducing him to a gambling den, an unfortunate development which coloured years of his working relationship with Lord Stanley, the future 14th Earl of Derby, and his predecessor as Conservative Prime Minister.

28–9

Contarini Fleming

16.5 x 19 cm, 4 volumes bound into two

32.182, pp. 72–3

In *Contarini Fleming*, published in February and May 1832, Disraeli returned to a familiar format, drawing on his geographic and psychological travels, interweaving them with Byronic associations. Byron's friends had included a Madame Contarini; there was a Doge named Contarini, and there are several palazzos with that name in and around Venice, a city with a special resonance in Disraeli's imagination. The Teutonic influences of Goethe's *Wilhelm Meister* are also evident.[4] But despite – or because of – the mix, the novel failed, making a profit of only £18. Its effect on the elderly writer William Beckford, however, was electric (see No. 38). Here he describes his meeting with a Turkish Military Commander.

72

found myself sleeping on the Divan, rolled up in its sacred carpet. The Bimbashee had wisely reeled to the fire. The thirst I felt was like that of Dives. All were sleeping except two, who kept up during the night the great wood fire. I rose, lightly stepping over my sleeping companions, and the shining arms that here and there informed me that the dark mass wrapped up in a capote was a human being. I found Abraham's bosom in a flagon of water. I think I must have drank a gallon at the draught. I looked at the wood fire, and thought of the blazing blocks in the Hall of Jonsterna, asked myself whether I were indeed in the mountain fastness of a Turkish chief, and shrugging my shoulders, went to sleep, and woke without a headache.

73

XII.

I PARTED from my jovial host the next morning very cordially, and gave him my pipe, as a memorial of having got tipsy together.

After having crossed one more range of steep mountains, we descended into a vast plain, over which we journeyed for some hours, the country presenting the same mournful aspect which I had too long observed : villages in ruins, and perfectly desolate—khans deserted, and fortresses rased to the ground—olive woods burnt up, and fruit trees cut down. So complete had been the work of destruction, that I often unexpectedly found my horse stumb

30
Standing for Parliament

22.5 x 18.5 cm
Dep. Hughenden 28/1, fol. 29ᵛ

Disraeli first stood for Parliament in June 1832 in the Wycombe by-election. Parliamentary immunity would protect him from creditors but Disraeli was also politically ambitious seeking, like Contarini, 'fame by devot[ing] myself to affairs' of state. But his political writings carried mixed signals. In Wycombe he stood as an independent Radical: the anti-reform Tories were a spent force and the Whigs, their French policy lashed by Disraeli in *Gallomania*, published in April, were far too aristocratic to admit him.

This second page of a letter from his cousin Ben Lindo describes unsuccessful attempts by Barnett to recruit Quaker voters. The Red Lion Inn (now demolished) was the scene of Disraeli's crowd-converting speech against his Whig opponent, Col. Grey, the Prime Minister's son, and ultimate victor with 20 of the 32 votes cast.

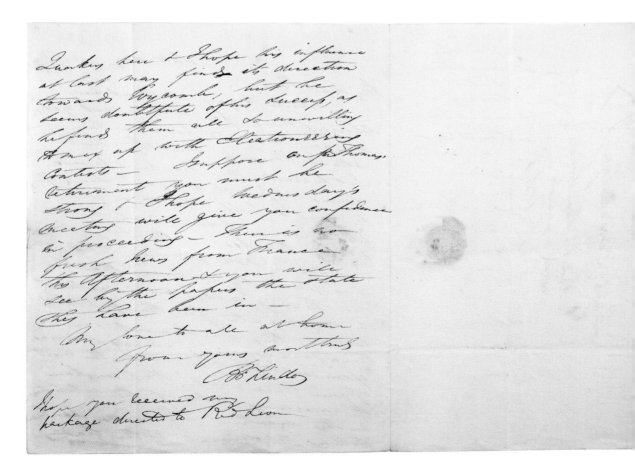

31
Reflections
18.5 x 23.5 cm
Dep. Hughenden 11/1/4, pp. 18–19

One of the most important documents in the Hughenden Papers is the Mutilated Diary, so-called because Disraeli subsequently excised some entries. The first pages describe the 1826 continental tour with the Austens but the reverse folios begin in 1833 and include such telling phrases as (p. 4), 'My life has not been a happy one – nature has given me an awful ambition and fiery passion. My life has been a struggle, with moments of rapture – a storm with dashes of moonlight…I struggle [p. 6] from Pride – Yes! it is Pride that now prompts me, not ambition – They shall not say I have failed…I have [pp. 18–19] an unerring instinct – I can read characters at a glance; few men can deceive me – my mind is a continental mind. It is a revolutionary mind – I am only truly great in action. If ever I am placed in a truly eminent position I shall prove this. I co[ul]d rule the House of Commons, altho' there wo[ul]d be a great prejudice against me at first.'

32
Bulwer Lytton condoles
22 x 14 cm
Dep. Hughenden 28/1, fol. 51

In this letter Bulwer Lytton sympathizes over the loss of Wycombe and encourages Disraeli to consider standing where two candidates could be returned for the same party (as was then possible); after several more unsuccessful attempts Disraeli would be returned in 1837 for just such a constituency: Maidstone. Disraeli greatly valued Bulwer's intellectually stimulating friendship. The satirical *Xion in Heaven*, published in Bulwer's *New monthly magazine* in December 1832 and February 1833, is considered one of Disraeli's most original works.

33–5
The two Henriettas: Lady Sykes & *Henrietta Temple:* A passionate encounter

33

23 x 19 cm
23 x 38 cm
Dep. Hughenden 13/1, fols. 80–1

In the summer of 1833 Disraeli met Sir Francis and Lady Sykes (d. 1846) and shortly afterwards began an affair with Henrietta. Sir Francis's property included Basildon Park in Berkshire (now a National Trust property), a setting for *Henrietta Temple*, the novel inspired by the affair and the pressing need to settle debts. Henrietta was aristocratic and sensuous and, as the references to 'A mother's kiss' (and overleaf, 'your faithful & fond love') indicate, capable of meeting Disraeli's complex emotional needs. Their relationship was aided by Sir Francis's frequent absences abroad and complicated in the summer of 1834 by Henrietta introducing Disraeli to his future mentor, the Lord Chancellor, Lord Lyndhurst (1772–1863) with whom she later became involved. But it would be her affair with Disraeli's friend, the painter Daniel Maclise, which ended their relationship in December 1836 and subsequently threatened Disraeli's future.

In 1838 Sir Francis sued Maclise for adultery and, until deterred by his solicitor, threatened to recover money he claimed had been improperly paid to Disraeli. It has been suggested that it was this money that helped to stave off Disraeli's bankruptcy at a critical time for him. In the Mutilated Diary entry for 1833 Disraeli attributed his 'happiest year' to being in love with Henrietta, the memories of this tenderness shaping his last letter to her in 1837 as her life fell apart.

This letter from Henrietta in August 1834 refers not only to the pain of separation but also to her pleasure that he is working on the novel, *Henrietta Temple*, and to her confidence that 'it will mend our broken fortune'. She continues 'Dearest my tears will blot the paper, & I cannot restrain them, I know not what I write'; not even detailing the latest society news helped: 'If you knew how desolate this [London] house is – your white stick on the sopha [sic], a ghost of departed joy'. We owe the survival of Henrietta's letters to Disraeli's literary executor, Montagu Corry.

34
Enraptured

Henrietta Temple (*a Love Story*) by the author of
Vivian Grey, published by Henry Colbourn,
London, 1837. Dedicated to The Count Alfred
D'Orsay by his affectionate friend.
19.2 x 23 cm
37.468 Vol. II, Book 3, pp. 10–11

Like her fictional counterpart, Lady Sykes would
ask herself whether regret mingled with remorse
for her love, but it would be in the context of her
affair with Maclise. As she wrote in her final letter
to Disraeli in July 1837, 'no one can reproach me of
anything but romantic folly'.⁵

CHAPTER II.
A DAY OF LOVE.

MEANWHILE the beautiful Henrietta sat in
her bower, her music neglected, her drawing
thrown aside. Even her birds were forgotten,
and her flowers untended. A soft tumult filled
her frame: now rapt in reverie she leaned her
head upon her fair hand in charmed abstraction;
now rising from her restless seat she paced the
chamber, and thought of his quick coming.
What was this mighty revolution that a few
short days—a few brief hours had occasioned?
How mysterious, yet how irresistible—how over-
whelming! Her father was absent, that father
on whose fond idea she had alone lived; from
whom the slightest separation had once been

pain; and now that father claims not even her
thoughts. Another, and a stranger's image, is
throned in her soul. She who had moved in the
world so variously—who had received so much
homage, and been accustomed from her childhood to all that is considered accomplished and
fascinating in man, and had passed through the
ordeal with a calm clear spirit; behold she is no
longer the mistress of her thoughts or feelings;
she had fallen before a glance, and yielded in an
instant to a burning word!

But could she blame herself? Did she repent
the rapid and ravishing past? Did regret mingle
with her wonder? Was there a pang of remorse,
however slight, blending its sharp tooth with all
her bliss? Oh! no! Her love was perfect, and
her joy was full. She offered her vows to that
heaven that had accorded her happiness so
supreme; she felt only unworthy of a destiny so
complete. She marvelled, in the meekness and
purity of her spirit, why one so gifted had been
reserved for her, and what he could recognise in

35
Lady Sykes

Lady Sykes by Daniel Maclise, RA, 1836
Original watercolour, 56 x 34 cm; reproduced by
permission of Sir John Sykes, Bt. and Professor
Elizabeth Sykes.

1834 was also significant for Disraeli's two
encounters with two of his predecessors as Prime
Minister – the Tory Duke of Wellington, who was
persuaded for political reasons to write in support
of his candidacy against the Liberal Grey, and
Lord Melbourne, then Home Secretary, who
would head the Whig administration. Disraeli's
conversation with the latter has become part of
the Disraeli legend. During a dinner party
Disraeli told Melbourne of his wish to be Prime
Minister one day and was advised to put such
nonsense out of his mind, which only increased
Disraeli's determination to achieve his goal.

36
Wycombe Re-visited

23.5 x 18.5 cm
Dep. Hughenden 28/1, fols. 98–99

At the turn of the year Disraeli, standing as an
Independent Radical again, unsuccessfully fought
Wycombe. The Duke of Wellington was
persuaded to write to the local grandee Lord
Carrington in support of Disraeli's anti-Whig
candidature for the borough of High Wycombe in
November but drew the line at meeting Disraeli.
Most of the letter discusses whether Parliament
will be dissolved, with only the briefest encouragement for Carrington to support Disraeli.
Having three times fought and lost as a Radical –
this time with the aid of Tory election funds
secured by Lord Lyndhurst – Disraeli soon moved
over to the Conservatives. The January 1835 result
in the two-member constituency was Robert
Smith (Whig) 289, Charles Grey (Whig) 147 and
Disraeli 128.

37

Vindication of the English Constitution (1835)

33.5 x 21.5 cm

Dep. Hughenden 217/3, fol. 167

In this two hundred and thirty-three page open letter to Lord Lyndhurst in December 1835 Disraeli outlined his alternative to the Whig interpretation of history, casting the Tories, not the Whigs – the authors of the 1832 Reform Bill – as the democratic, majority, national party. Inspired by the eighteenth-century Lord Bolingbroke's view of conservatism and his own fascination with English history and the aristocracy (and indebted to Edmund Burke's writings), Disraeli began to develop his interpretation of conservatism: the vision of an outsider with a reverence for British institutions, the

Monarchy, the House of Lords and the Church, yet infused with radicalism. This outlook he explored further in his novels. The *Vindication* earned praise from both its dedicatee and Peel, the Party leader.

This page opens with the observation that 'The great art in creating an efficient Representative Government is to secure representation of those interests of the country which are at one and the same time not only considerable but in their nature permanent.' The work also pointed towards universal suffrage.

38

Beckford regenerated

18.2 x 11 cm
18.2 x 22.5 cm
MS. Beckford c. 29, fols. 100–1

Disraeli's encounter with William Beckford (1760–1844), the author and aesthete, was not so much a stepping stone in his own life as a vital boost to the elderly writer's creativity. Beckford had been impressed by *Contarini Fleming* and *Alroy*. *Henrietta Temple* was less to his taste and his words of praise about the book appear never to have reached Disraeli. Disraeli's friendship with Beckford, conducted by letter with only one meeting face-to-face, energized the latter, encouraging him to work again.

(See Timothy Mowl, 'Disraeli's novels and the Beckford connection', pp. 29–34.) For his part Disraeli was pleased to know a man of 'the greatest taste'. In this draft letter to Disraeli Beckford regrets that he had not received a copy of the newly-published *Venetia* and appears to have some difficulty finding the right words to close the letter.

TO THE

FREEMEN

AND

ELECTORS

OF THE

BOROUGH OF

MAIDSTONE.

GENTLEMEN;

Having now completed the Canvass of the Borough, and received promises of support from yourselves which render our return as your Representatives in the ensuing Parliament, as far as human causes can operate, no longer a matter of doubt, we beg to offer you our cordial acknowledgment of the generous reception which we have experienced, and to express our readiness and resolution to afford you, at the proper time, an opportunity, if necessary, of recording your suffrages.

We have earnestly endeavoured to pay our personal respects to every Elector, and if we have not always been successful, we trust we shall be more fortunate before the day of election arrives.

We solicit your confidence as upholders of that Protestant Constitution to which we are indebted for the civil and religious liberty which has long been the boast of Britons, and as opposers of that heartless system of legislation which would degrade the still free, though humbler, subjects of the realm in the scale of society. It will be our object to resist that Liberalism in politics, which it seems, is only another phrase for an attack upon the Protestant Religion and the English Poor.

Although, we trust, our loyalty to our Sovereign will never be questioned, we deem it our duty explicitly to state, that we have no confidence in the weak and inefficient Ministry with which circumstances have trammelled our Queen. They have contrived at the same time to derange the credit, to sully the honor, and to disturb the order of the realm, and are now avowedly leagued with those who aim at its subversion.

ELECTORS OF MAIDSTONE! the struggle is rapidly approaching. The glory of the country and the prosperity of all classes of her Majesty's subjects depend upon the result. Who, then, can doubt its character? You, among the rest, will do your duty, and we shall endeavour to do ours.

We remain,

Gentlemen,

Your obliged and faithful Servants,

WYNDHAM LEWIS,
B. DISRAELI.

Maidstone,
July 8th, 1837.

PRINTED BY J. V. HALL AND SON, KING'S ARMS OFFICE, HIGH-STREET, MAIDSTONE.

39
Election address, 1837
45.5 x 38.5 cm
Dep. Hughenden 28/4, fol. 5

Disraeli was finally elected to the House of Commons in July 1837, when he was returned as one of the two Conservative candidates for the Kent constituency of Maidstone, in the General Election called after the accession of Queen Victoria to the throne. The fact that the other candidate, Wyndham Lewis (1780–1838), was the husband of Disraeli's future wife, Mary Anne, imbues the event with longer-term emotional significance. More prosaically Disraeli was finally beyond the reach of his creditors, though not the necessity of rescheduling his debts. This address drafted, with very few revisions, by Disraeli, includes references to upholding the Protestant constitution, opposing the Poor Law and freeing the Monarchy from the 'trammels' of the Whig Government.

40

Maiden speech
Doulton Commemorative jug, made in Lambeth,
London, [for] John Mortlock, Oxford Street,
London.
17 x 12 cm
Lent by a private collector

On 7 December 1837 Disraeli made his parliamentary debut. Characteristically he wanted to make his mark immediately. But his choice of topic, Irish elections, was highly unwise, as was his timing: the previous speaker was Daniel O'Connell (1775–1847) leader of the Irish MPs. In May 1835 during the Taunton by-election Disraeli had been involved in a ferocious quarrel with O'Connell over the latter's new alliance with the Whigs and Disraeli's move to the Conservatives. After O'Connell's inflammatory comments about Disraeli's lineage Disraeli challenged O'Connell's son to a duel, but ended up being bound over to keep the peace.

His maiden speech was met with derision and not only by the Irish MPs; his convoluted style of delivery compounded his difficulties. Most of his speech was inaudible over the din but his closing remarks, 'Though I sit down now the time will come when you will hear me' were prophetic. Disraeli learnt from his failure and took the advice of an Irish MP with little enthusiasm for O'Connell, Richard O'Shiel (1794–1851): 'Get rid of your Genius for a session. Speak often for you should not show yourself cowed, but speak shortly… try to be dull… and in a short time the House will sigh for [your] wit and eloquence.'[6]

CHAPTER FOUR

1837–45

Mary Anne, Young England, and the Trilogy

Mary Anne

ALTHOUGH DISRAELI achieved his ambition to enter Parliament in 1837, married, and wrote a novel which included one of the most famous descriptions in nineteenth-century literature (the rich and the poor in *Sybil or two nations*) this period was not without its frustrations. As his thirties slipped into his forties the realities of his situation fell short of the greatness to which he still aspired.

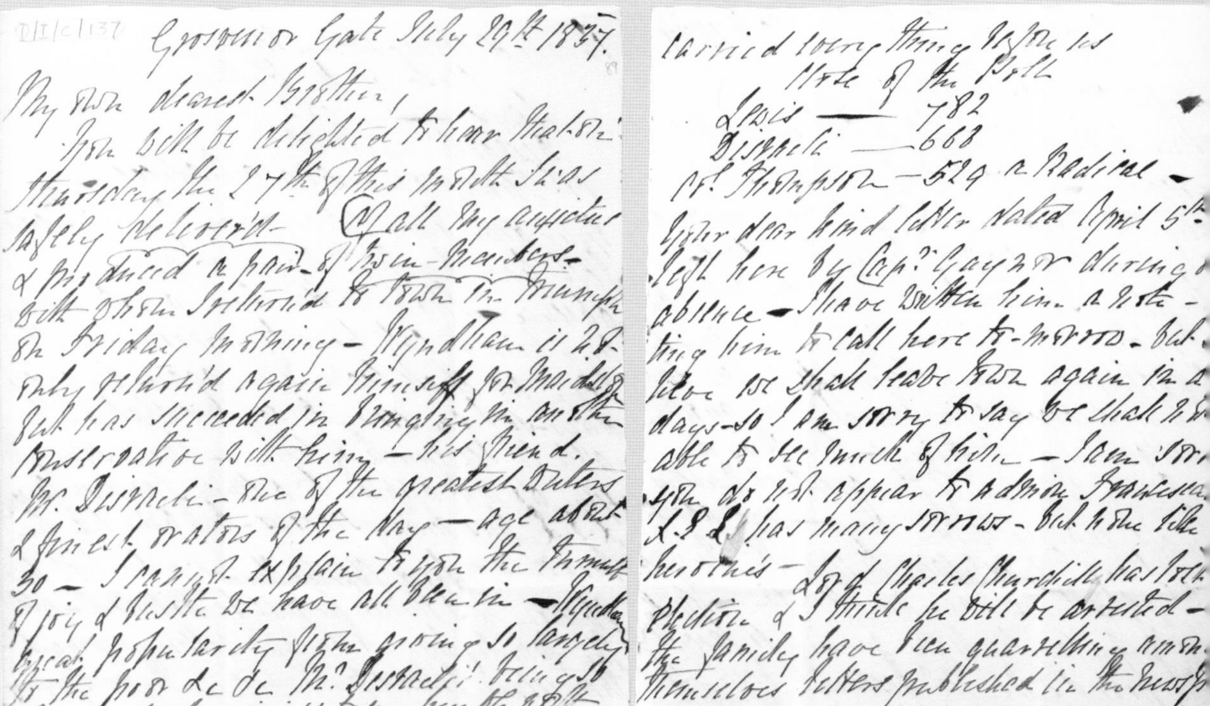
D/I/C/137 Grosvenor Gate July 29th 1837.
My own dearest Brother,
You will be delighted to hear that on Thursday the 27th of this month I was safely delivered — after all my anxieties & produced a pair of twin Members — with whom I returned to town in triumph on Friday morning — Wyndham is not only returned again himself for Maidstone but has succeeded in bringing in another conservative with him — his friend Mr. Disraeli — one of the greatest writers & finest orators of the day — age about 30 — I cannot explain to you the triumph of joy & bustle we have all been in — Wyndham's great popularity & then giving so largely to the poor &c &c Mr. Disraeli being so fine a speaker joined to my humble self

carried everything before us
State of the Poll
Lewis — 782
Disraeli — 668
Col. Thompson — 529 a Radical —
Your dear kind letter dated April 5th left here by Capt. Gaynor during our absence — I have written him a note inviting him to call here to-morrow — but alas we shall leave town again in a few days — so I am sorry to say we shall not be able to see much of him — I am sorry you do not appear to admire [illegible] L.E.L. has many sorrows — but [illegible] heroines — Lord Charles Churchill has lost his election & I think he will be arrested — the family have been quarrelling among themselves letters published in the newsp[illegible]

41

Mary Anne's prophecy

23 x 19 cm

Dep. Hughenden 169/4, fols. 89ʳ–90ᵛ

Famously described by Disraeli to Sarah as a 'flirt and a rattle' after their first meeting in 1832, Mary Anne Lewis's assessment of her future husband was more profound. In this letter to her brother John Evans (d. 1858), written from the Lewis home in London's Grosvenor Gate on 29 July 1837, she refers (fol. 89) to Wyndham Lewis's electoral success with 'his friend Mr Disraeli', overrating him as 'one of the greatest writers &

finest orators of the day – age about 30'; lists the result (fol. 89ᵛ) 'Lewis 782, Disraeli 668, Col Thompson 529 a Radical', adds some further observations and ends tellingly (fol. 90ᵛ) 'Mark what I say – Mark what I Prophecy [sic] – Mr Disraeli will, in very few years, be one of the greatest men of his day – his great talents back'd by his friends Lord Lyndhurst & Lord Chandos…' (later 2ⁿᵈ Duke of Buckingham).

42

Courtship

22.5 x 37 cm

Dep. Hughenden 1/2, fols. 52–3

Initially attracted by Mary Anne's wealth and the political necessity of having a wife, Disraeli was not deflected when he discovered that Mary Anne only had a life interest in her late husband's money. Her income was a factor as it boosted his credit-worthiness, but Disraeli tried – as he had with his father – to conceal the scale of his indebtedness from her. Ultimately about £13,000 (today's £65,000) of her income was used for his debts (in 1841 these stood at £20,000, much of it due to interest and poor debt management).

At least twelve years older than Disraeli, shrewd yet prone to social gaffes, Mary Anne's emotional support was important to Disraeli. In this letter, written from Bradenham in October 1838 while he was writing *Alarcos* (a poem which he hoped to see staged), Disraeli professes the strength of his feelings for Mary Anne, salutes her inspirational role, envies three (assumed) rivals for her affections and breaks into verse. (Published as Letter 827 in *Benjamin Disraeli Letters Volume III: 1838–41* (Toronto, 1987).)

43
'Mrs Disraeli'
Miniature of Mary Anne by Francis Rochard
30.5 x 22.5 cm

Reproduced by permission of Hughenden Manor
(The National Trust).

45
Young Disraeli
Watercolour by Dighton *c.*1840
42 x 32 cm

A restrained-looking Disraeli. The bright colours
and curls are gone. He adopted this sober 'look'
for the rest of his life.
Reproduced by permission of the John Murray
Archive.

44

The Disraeli marriage

22.5 x 18.5 cm, A4

Dep. Hughenden 4/2, fols. 186–7 and transcript

Perhaps the secret of the success of the Disraeli marriage lay in their contrasting qualities, as outlined here by Mary Anne (represented in the right-hand column). They were married on 27 August 1839; Lord Lyndhurst was the Best Man.

If Disraeli strayed – and he is reputed to have done so after the marriage moved towards its second decade – any evidence would have been removed by his executor, Sir Philip Rose, when he weeded the papers after Disraeli's death.

List of qualities made by the future Mrs. Disraeli (1839)

'His eyes they are as black as Sloes, But oh! So beautiful his nose'

Very Calm	Very effervescent
Manners grave and almost sad	Gay and happy looking when speaking
Never irritable	Very irritable
Bad-humoured	Good-humoured
Warm in love but cold in friendship	Cold in love but warm in friendship
Very patient	No patience
Very studious	Very idle
Very generous	Only generous to those she loves
Often says what he does not think	Never says anything she does not think
It is impossible to find out who he likes or dislikes from his manner. He does not show his feelings	Her manner is quite different, and to those she likes she shows her feelings
No vanity	Much vanity
Conceited	No conceit
No self-love	Much self-love
He is seldom amused	Everything amuses her
He is a genius	She is a dunce
He is to be depended on to a certain degree	She is not to be depended on
His whole soul is devoted to politics and ambition	She has no ambition and hates politics

So it is evident they sympathise only on one subject: Maidstone like most husbands and wives about their Children.

Young England

DISAPPOINTED WITH his lack of progress in Peel's Government (his early request for office was rebuffed), Disraeli became leader of the Young England group, all of whom had been elected by 1842. Here was another small group of aristocratic rebels, principally focused on George Smythe and Lord John Manners, Alexander Cochrane-Baillie and Richard Monckton Milnes (see No. 67), with whom Disraeli could identify. Their youth and admiration added to their appeal for him. Young England, like the Oxford Movement, faced the present by looking towards the distant past for inspiration and direction.

The group dissolved over the Maynooth Grant in 1845 – the same issue over which Gladstone resigned from the Cabinet – but their significance reaches beyond their opposition to Peel's policies and the erosion of aristocratic power. They later provided the model for the Fourth Party in the late 1870s led by Lord Randolph Churchill (1849–94) and the Primrose League founded by the Conservatives in 1883 in response to the extension of the (male) franchise.

46
George Smythe

21 x 13.7 cm

Dep. Hughenden 144/1, fols. 227–8

George Smythe, later 7th Viscount Strangford
(1818–57), was the highly idealized model for the
eponymous hero in *Coningsby* and Waldershare in
Endymion. Here Smythe writes in November 1842
with youthful exuberance, and more than a hint of
delight in the chase and in backbench intrigue,
about the prospects for damaging Peel, urging
Disraeli to write 'something <u>presuming</u> a split in
the ranks of the Ministerialism [sic] … don't let
us lie behind our ancestors in courage or wit!' But
when Disraeli destroyed Peel in 1846 Smythe, by
then a junior minister in the Foreign Office,
remained a Peelite supporter. Disraeli, alive to
Smythe's limitations, had nevertheless encouraged
him as a potential leader and as a writer but it was
as a leader writer for the *Morning Chronicle* that
he later excelled before dying young.[7]

47
Lord John Manners

18.3 x 22.7 cm

Dep. Hughenden 106/1, fols. 10ʳ–11

Lord John Manners, later 7th Duke of Rutland
(1818–1906), regarded by Disraeli as a future Prime
Minister, risked the wrath of his father by allying
with Disraeli, though he stopped short of total
defiance. Smythe's best friend at Cambridge, he
was the model for Lord Henry Sidney in
Coningsby. Disinclined to attend a proposed
public meeting in Birmingham – 'at Christmas
time one ought to be at home, and really we have
had enough of public meetings for one winter' –
he reports in this October 1844 letter (fol. 10ᵛ) on
the response of the gentry to their movement.
Henry Lyster had criticized Disraeli's speech at
Shrewsbury (Disraeli's constituency, 1841–7)
without hearing it. Manners, with his interest in
factory reform and allotments, moves on to
compare English and Irish peasants and their
holdings and the views of Sir Edwin Chadwick
(1800–90), the great sanitary reformer.

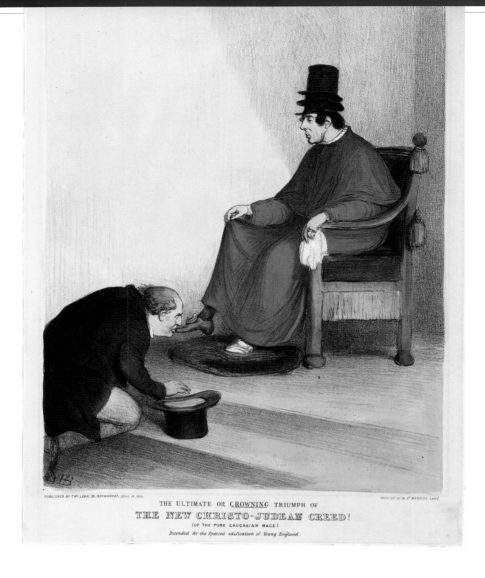

PUBLISHED BY T. MC LEAN, 26. HAYMARKET, JUNE 14, 1844.   PRINTED AT 25. ST MARTINS LANE

THE ULTIMATE OR CROWNING TRIUMPH OF
THE NEW CHRISTO-JUDEAN CREED!
(OF THE PURE CAUCASIAN RACE)
Intended for the Special edification of Young England.

48

Political Cartoon

*The Ultimate or Crowning Triumph of the new
Christo-Judean creed (of the pure Caucasian race)
Inscribed for special edification of Young England* by
HB, published by T. Maclean, London 1844.
34.6 x 25.8 cm
John Johnson Political Cartoons 6 (223)

This cartoon can be interpreted on several
levels, none of which is flattering to Disraeli.
His views on religion are ridiculed, his true
ambitions questioned and, in a none-too-subtle
way, the once familiar dandyish ringlets are re-
styled. Young England is warned off. Disraeli
was regularly depicted in cartoons many of
which, like 'Old Clothes', were openly anti-
Semitic. The spoof play bill (see No. 136) is in a
similar vein. Such negative images may have
contributed to his 'Sphinx'-like, stoical public
persona.

The Trilogy

IN THE MID-1840s Disraeli returned to novel-writing to explore his political and social ideas. Two novels, *Coningsby* (1844) and *Sybil* (1845), appeared in quick succession; the third, *Tancred* (1847), was delayed by the campaign against Peel.

49

Coningsby, or the New Generation

World Classic's edition (1932) of the 1844 work, with introduction by André Maurois, author of *La Vie de Disraëli* (Paris, 1928).

15 x 17.5 cm

256 f. 2750, pp. 220–1

Coningsby, widely regarded as the first political novel, was begun in the summer of 1843 while Disraeli, who had just openly opposed Peel over a measure for Ireland, was staying at Deepdene with Henry Hope (to whom the book was dedicated) and the Byronic Smythe, who had also gone there to write. Set at the time of the 1832 Reform Bill, the book is peopled with real and imagined figures. Its ambitious aim was to explore the 'derivation and character of political parties', the resulting condition of the people and the Church's remedial role, though only the first theme was covered.[8] Coningsby's mentor is Sidonia – another of Disraeli's idealized self-portraits, linked to his imagined Venetian past; the fictional relationship again symbolizing a beneficial connection between Judaism and Christianity. In this extract (p. 220) Sidonia questions whether the extension of the franchise was the best guarantee of representation and (p. 221) enthuses about the new generation, the fictional equivalents of Young England.

50

Sybil or the two nations **By Benjamin
Disraeli MP, author of Coningsby** (second
edition) Henry Colburn, 1845, Vol. 3, pp. 148–9
18.9 x 22.5 cm
Vet. A6 e.18/1

Perhaps Disraeli's best-known novel, with its
reference to the existence of two nations, the rich
and poor living side by side but in two separate
worlds, 'ignorant of each other's habits, thoughts
and feelings'. For his description of social
conditions Disraeli drew on primary and secondary
sources and his own observations. With its
rejection of materialism and emphasis on social
welfare *Sybil* is perhaps also his most idealistic
work. It did not propose specific remedies but its
resonance lasted well beyond the 1840s. After the
Second World War some of the brightest of the
new parliamentary intake would form the One
Nation Group. *Sybil* was dedicated to Mary Anne.
Published like *Coningsby* in three volumes it, too,
sold 3,000 copies. Both novels made about £1,000
profit each, which Disraeli and Colburn shared
equally.

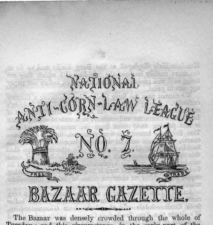

51

An alternative vision
National Anti-Corn Law League Bazaar Gazette
No. 7 (1845)
John Johnson Free Trade & Protection Box 5

Two great reform movements, the Chartists and
the Anti-Corn Law League, helped to shape the
political climate in the 1840s. This publication,
designed to keep the League's supporters
informed on the latest developments, describes a
week-long national free trade bazaar held in
London in 1845. The celebration of manufactured
goods, the support for free trade and the shift in
economic power pointed to the future, but the
repeal of the Corn Laws would shatter the unity
of the Tories under Peel.

52
'Mary Anne, Viscountess Beaconsfield' by
J. G. Middleton
Oil on canvas, 114.3 x 88.9 cm, reproduced by
permission of Hughenden Manor (The National
Trust).

53
**George Smythe, later 7th Viscount
Strangford** (1818–57) by R. Buckner, n.d.
Oil on canvas, 86.4 x 61 cm, reproduced by
permission of Hughenden Manor (The National
Trust).

54
**Lord John Manners, later 7th Duke of
Rutland** (1818–1906), after Sir Francis Grant,
PRA, n.d.
Oil on canvas, 114.3 x 79 cm, reproduced by
permission of Hughenden Manor (The National
Trust).

55
Sir Robert Peel (1788–1850)
Engraving by W. Holl from Cabinet picture by
Thomas Lawrence, in Alexander Ewald, *The Rt.
Hon. Benjamin Disraeli, Earl of Beaconsfield, K.G.
and his times*, Vol. II (London, 1881–4).
210 h.328e

57

Hughenden Manor, South Front

Photograph; reproduced by permission of
Hughenden Manor (The National Trust).
The neo-Jacobean exterior dates from the
remodelling of a Georgian house in 1862–3 by the
architect E. B. Lamb (1806–69). It was financed
by Mary Anne's money and the prospect of the
Brydges Willyams legacy.

56

Edward Stanley, 14th Earl of Derby (1799–
1869) by Jane Hawkins, after Sir Francis Grant,
PRA.

Oil on canvas, 86.5 x 61 cm, reproduced by
permission of Hughenden Manor (The National
Trust).

A Sketch taken at Torquay. Devon in 1853

Mrs Brydges Williams of Broddon Hill, Torquay. Devon. The Lady benefactress who bequeathed the Earl ~ Beaconsfield. Fifty thousand pounds. with Mansion Plate. Old China. Jewels &c.

58
Mrs Brydges Willyams (d. 1863)
Sketch, 5.5 x 6.8 cm, taken at Torquay, Devon, 1853.
MS. Eng. lett. d. 340

59
Mary Anne's house
Print by Barbara Jones, 25 x 18.5 cm in *Recording Britain,* Vol. 1, (1946).

The house, 1 Grosvenor Gate / 93 Park Lane, occupying a corner site on Park Lane in London's Mayfair, is one of a bow-fronted group dating from 1823–7. It is only eight doors up from the family home of Sir Robert Peel in Upper Grosvenor Street. The two houses would have witnessed very different responses to the fall of Peel's government in 1846.

CHAPTER FIVE

1846–9

Tumultuous Times

DISRAELI WAS a major player in the downfall of Sir Robert Peel. Peel's rejection of the Corn Laws, to which he had committed the Party in the 1841 election, and his moves towards Free Trade and a more liberal conservatism, provoked the Protectionist faction. The Corn Laws were especially emotive because of the links between protecting British agricultural interests, taxing cheaper imports, and the cost of the domestic loaf. Peel's proposal to repeal the Corn Laws as famine swept Ireland – and all that it symbolized – was hugely divisive. Writing in the mid-1960s, Lord Blake has compared the divisiveness to that of two twentieth-century benchmarks, the Abdication crisis and Munich. To these one might add the Suez crisis, the Falklands war and more recent crises. But it was not the only issue troubling Peel's relations with his party.

Ambitious to make his mark, and influenced by a romantic political attachment to the aristocratic settlement, Disraeli spearheaded the Protectionist faction, arguing against total repeal rather than for protectionism. If the leaders thought they could discard him after the battle they underestimated his tenacity.

60

The Rising Generation – in Parliament
Cartoon No. 3 in *The Earl of Beaconsfield K.G. Cartoons from "Punch", 1843–1878* (1878)
29 x 22 cm
Johnson d. 4932

The magazine *Punch* clearly didn't have a very high opinion of Disraeli's intentions.

61

'The fall of Caesar – not that I have loved Caesar less'
Coloured print, 29.5 x 37.6 cm, published by Thomas Maclean, London, 18 July 1846.
John Johnson Political cartoons 6 (257)

A shocked Caesar/Peel is ambushed by his critics: Bentinck, Cobden, O'Connell, Lord John Russell, Morpeth, Palmerston, Shiel and a sword-wielding Disraeli. A graphic illustration of events prefigured in Disraeli's correspondence with Young England (and encouraged by Bentinck, shown here with a dagger), but it is Disraeli's opportunism which is remembered. Lord Derby would later explain it to Queen Victoria as the trait of a man who had to make his own way.

62

Disraeli, the Protectionists and the fall of Peel
18 x 11.3 cm
Dep. Hughenden 89/1, fols. 3–4, 6–7ᵛ

This ten-page letter in April 1846 from the new Leader of the Protectionists – Lord George Bentinck, a Norfolk MP and racing enthusiast (1802–48) – begins by referring to Ireland before moving on to the position of farmers without capital, the responses of the Dominions to free trade on timber, and Protectionist tactics; but perhaps the most telling phrase urges Disraeli 'to drive well into Peel's vitals'.

In the spring of 1846 the Conservative Party imploded. Disraeli's relentless parliamentary attacks on Peel since January and his partnership with Bentinck undermined the Premier as he tried to carry the party in favour of the repeal of the Corn Laws to ease the Irish famine, and to introduce a coercion bill to deal with rioting in Ireland. The willingness of the Whigs and Radicals to support the former but reject the latter added to Peel's difficulties and ultimate resignation in June. The party split in two: the minority Peelites taking the majority of the party's leaders (with all the organization and funding) and the Protectionists. It would be nearly thirty years before the realigned Conservatives formed a majority government.

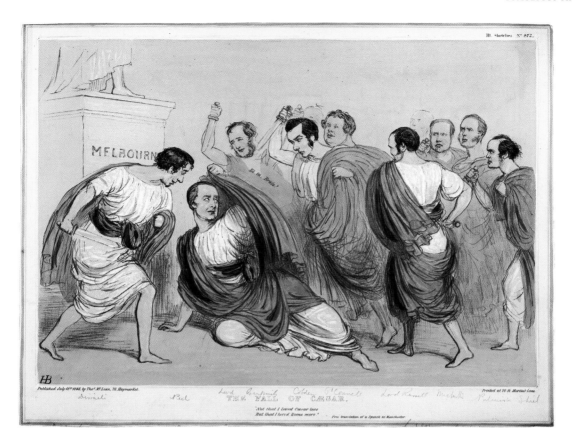

THE FALL OF CÆSAR.

63
'The Ministry has resigned'

18 x 11; 18 x 22 cm

Dep. Hughenden 2/2, fols. 42ʳ, 42ᵛ–43ʳ

'All Coningsby and Young England the general exclamation here', as Disraeli excitedly wrote to his wife. Disraeli relished being the focus of attention, combining his political and literary skills, propelling events – and himself – forward. In 1862, writing to Samuel Wilberforce, Disraeli would allude to the 'unhappy consequences of the unfortunate disruption of 1846' adding, characteristically, that like many others 'equally inconvenient, time would cure [them]'.[9]

64

Biographical tool

Lord George Bentinck: a political biography, revised,
3rd edition published by Colburn & Co., London,
1852.

24 x 21 cm

2288 e.1337, pp. 332–3

Partnership with Bentinck Disraeli's ended when
Bentinck resigned as leader of the Protectionists
in December 1847 and died, unexpectedly, in 1848.
Bentinck had supported Lord Granby as his
successor. Hostility towards Disraeli within the
Protectionist leadership (including Lord Stanley
and the party whips) further blocked his
succession, which after a hiatus passed to Lord
Stanley (after the death of his father, in 1851,
known as Lord Derby), who sat in the House of
Lords. Derby, like Bentinck, overcame his dislike
and distrust of Disraeli.

In the Bentinck biography Disraeli set out his
version of events using the opportunity to modify
Derby's stand on protection, making it easier for
the party to abandon it. He was also moved to
devote a whole chapter to 'The Jewish Question',
sandwiching it – rather oddly – between that on
the panic of 1847 and Bentinck's accession to the
leadership, and emphasizing the significance of
the Jewish inspiration to Christianity and
Europe's artistic development. The figure
described on this page is more an amalgam of
Bentinck and Disraeli than pure Bentinck.

332   A POLITICAL BIOGRAPHY.

CHAPTER XIX.

IF we take a general view of the career of Lord
George Bentinck during the last seven months—from
the time indeed when he was trying to find a lawyer
to convey his convictions to the house of commons
until the moment when her majesty prorogued her parliament, the results will be found to be very remarkable.   So much was never done so unexpectedly
by any public man in the same space of time.   He
had rallied a great party which seemed hopelessly
routed ; he had established a parliamentary disci-
pline in their ranks which old political connections
led by experienced statesmen have seldom surpassed ;
he had brought forward from those ranks entirely
through his discrimination and by his personal encouragement considerable talents in debate ; he had
himself proved a master in detail and in argument of
all the great questions arising out of the reconstruc-

A POLITICAL BIOGRAPHY.   333

tion of our commercial system ; he had made a vindication of the results of the protective principle as
applied to agriculture which certainly so far as the
materials are concerned, is the most efficient plea
that ever was urged in the house of commons in
favour of the abrogated law ; he had exhibited similar
instances of investigation in considerable statements
with respect to the silk trade and other branches of
our industry ; he had asserted the claims of the productive classes in Ireland and in our timber and
sugar producing colonies with the effect which results from a thorough acquaintance with a subject ;
he had promulgated distinct principles with regard
to our financial as well as to our commercial system ;
he had maintained the expediency of relieving the
consumer by the repeal of excise in preference to
customs' duties, and of establishing fiscal reciprocity as
a condition of mercantile exchange.   On subjects of
a more occasional but analogous nature he had
shown promptitude and knowledge, as in the instances of the urgent condition of Mexico and of our
carrying trade with the Spanish colonies, both of
which he brought forward in the last hours of the
session, but the importance of which motions was
recognised by all parties.   Finally, he had attracted
the notice and in many instances obtained the confidence of large bodies of men in the country, who
recognised in him a great capacity of labour com-

65

Confidential man of business

18 x 11; 18 x 22 cm

Dep. Hughenden 307/1, fols. 7–8

'I want a confidential man of business in whose talents, zeal & fidelity, I can repose a complete trust': so wrote Disraeli in April 1846 to Philip – later Sir Philip – Rose (1816–83), a lawyer specializing in electoral litigation. 'The pressure of public life has become so extreme… that I can no longer attend to my private affairs…'[10] Disraeli had known Rose, the son of the D'Israelis' doctor at Bradenham, for some while. This marks a new departure. Rose was entrusted with raising the £25,000 Disraeli needed to add to his own £10,000 to purchase the Hughenden estate and – among other things – dealing with his still-problematic finances. In this letter written on 6 December 1846 Disraeli alludes to the valuation of the estate timber.

66

The Bentincks and the acquisition of Hughenden

18 x 11.3 cm

Dep. Hughenden 89/1, fols. 145–50

Bentinck had pledged a loan of £25,000 towards the purchase of the 750-acre Hughenden estate which his family honoured after his death. Hughenden, finally acquired in 1848, was in effect Disraeli's constituency home – he was returned for Buckinghamshire in 1847. It connected him to the county network on the scale essential for major political figures right down to the last century. The Liberal H. H. Asquith (1852–1928), Prime Minister 1908–16, was the first not to own land. Disraeli had invented his own aristocratic past, defended and written about the British aristocracy, and moved in aristocratic circles; now he was living his dream. (See Roland Quinault, 'Disraeli and Buckinghamshire', pp. 35–43.)

67

The trilogy completed: *Tancred* and Disraeli's orientalism

20.5 x 12.7 cm; 33 x 20.4 cm

MS. Berlin 484, fol. 7^r; MS. Berlin 485, fol. 128^r

The campaign against Peel prevented Disraeli completing the final book in his trilogy. In *Tancred*, which appeared in 1847, Disraeli resumes his 'creative' role – for him an indispensable aspect of politics – and explores his views on race and religion, drawing once more on his youthful travels in the east. The earlier chapters, set in London, provide the social comedy. A Young England figure again inspires a major character: this time it is Richard Monckton Milnes (later Baron Houghton, 1809–85) as Mr Vavasour – much to Milnes's irritation, as his critical review of the trilogy attested.

Sir Isaiah Berlin (1909–97), the noted philosopher and historian of ideas, was one of the first writers to address the issue of Disraeli's Jewishness. His lecture 'Benjamin Disraeli, Karl Marx and the search for Identity', delivered to the Jewish Historical Society in 1967, is masterly. In these extracts from a draft and a notebook in the Berlin papers, Sir Isaiah places *Tancred* in the context of Disraeli's orientalism and self-image.

- 18 -

basis of all subsequent civilized society. They worshipped its literature, its sabbath, the sacred history of the Jewish people, the hymns, laments and praises, finally, "the son of a Jewish woman as their God" "Yet, nevertheless they excluded with disdain from their society and their parliament, as if they were the off-scourings of the earth, the race to which they owed their festivals, their psalms, their semi-civilization, their religion and their God. He racked his brains".

I need not remind you of all the passages quoted by Disraeli's many biographers, particularly the Jews among them, of all those lyrical outbursts in which he speaks of the ancient Hebrews and of the Jews in general. In his early fantasy "The Wondrous Tale of Alroy" the hero restores the Jews to their ancient land, conquers the whole of Asia minor, and finally perishes in glorious fashion. In Coningsby, the mysterious and omnipotent figure of Sidonia, benevolent, powerful, all but omniscient, is a representative of the "pure Asian breed" that makes Jews and Arabs cousins and causes Disraeli to describe the Arabs as merely "Jews on horseback". Sidonia explains that the Jews have triumphed over time and persecution because of their "Caucasian blood", and the wise laws that segregate them from lower races. He compares them favourably with "some flat-nosed Frank, full of bustle, and puffed-up with self-conceit (a race, spawned perhaps in the morasses of some northern forest, hardly yet cleared.)" There is a   vision of Lothair. There are the fantastic scenes in Tancred when "The Angel of Arabia" addresses the hero in Palestine in mystical words. This novel, Disraeli's favourite, is

CHAPTER SIX

1849–59

Moving on, Moving up

THESE TEN YEARS saw Disraeli become leader of the Conservatives in the House of Commons and his appointment as Chancellor of the Exchequer. One of the most unusual aspects is the triangular relationship between Disraeli, Lord Stanley (who became the 14th Earl of Derby in 1851), the leader of the party overall, and his son Lord Stanley (the 15th Earl of Derby after 1869). When Derby led the minority Conservative Governments in 1852 and 1858–9, Disraeli served as Chancellor of the Exchequer. In Disraeli's 1868 Government and for most of that of 1874–8 Derby's son was Foreign Secretary. The relations between the Prime Minister, the Chancellor and the Foreign Secretary are crucial in government but here the personal mix was even more complex. (See Angus Hawkins, 'Disraeli and the Earls of Derby', pp. 16-20.)

20 March 1849. I returned from America. Found my father,[1] by his account, ready to take office. He however feared that ministers would resign in order to force him into power prematurely. He wished for delay, as tending to heal past wounds, and reunite the party.

He repeated a conversation between himself and Mr Disraeli[2] on the subject of the leadership. He proposed the triumvirate as now existing (Herries,[3] Granby,[4] Disraeli). D. refused. My Father reminded him of his offer to act with Lord George Bentinck[5] under Granby. 'It is quite true' D. said 'that I acceded to such an arrangement when acting in union, and on terms of equality with, Lord George Bentinck: but I am Disraeli the adventurer and I will not acquiesce in a position which will enable the party to make use of me in debate, and then throw me aside.' My Father replied that the lead of the Commons was a question to be decided by the party in that house, and not by him: they had raised strong objections to Mr D. being sole leader, and he could not in such a matter attempt to coerce them.

Mr D. then declined all interference in party arrangements and said that he should be happy to give an independent support, but that he would speak only when it suited him as a private member. He wished to retire, and devote at least part of his time to literature.

'All this is very well' my Father answered 'but the position is one which you cannot hold. Peel[6] has tried it, and you see how his influence is gone. Your proposal, if it means anything, means that we are to lose you altogether.'

Mr D. thanked Lord Stanley for speaking so frankly, but said his mind was made up. My Father determined, as he told me, to try once more. He represented that Mr D. must be himself aware of the impossibility of acting alone. 'I would not apply to you any such terms as you have applied to yourself: but this I will say, that certain feelings exist, call them prejudices if you will, that will make many of our friends desire, in the man who is to lead them, a degree of station and influence which circumstances have not as yet enabled you to acquire: and if I were speaking to an ambitious man, and speaking for your interest alone, I tell you fairly, I could suggest no proposal which I think you would gain more by accepting. You escape the envy which attaches to a post of solitary and supreme command; you are associated with two men, neither of whom in point of abilities can stand in your way for a moment: but one of whom possesses a station and a private character which will ensure him support, while, so far from being ambitious of power, he has refused the lead when pressed upon him. The other is an

1

68
Leader of the Party in the Commons

18 x 11.2; 18 x 22.4 cm
Dep. Hughenden 109/1, fols. 12–15

Many of the letters of Lord Stanley exceed twelve pages but this relatively short one of six pages was written from his country house, Knowsley Hall, in January 1849. Disraeli had written that he would prefer to withdraw rather than give way to another member becoming Leader of the Conservatives in the Commons. Disraeli lacked widespread support, but he was not without supporters and his skills were badly needed in the party. Stanley pitched his letter cleverly, emphasizing the responsibilities they both shared: 'I feel that I – and excuse me if I add that you – cannot so withdraw. He who has once put his hand to the Parliamentary plough cannot draw back.'

69
The Younger Stanley's perspective

Disraeli, Derby and the Conservative Party: Journals of Edward Henry Lord Stanley, 1849–1869, edited by John Vincent (Hassocks, 1978), pp. 1–3
2288 d.613

These March 1849 entries in the diaries of Lord Stanley reveal that three months later the issue was still unresolved. Disraeli may have agreed to share power but he had no intention of making the arrangement work. Stanley continued to consult Lord Granby – later 6th Duke of Rutland (1815–88) – often ahead of as well as alongside Disraeli, but the latter was effectively leader in the Commons, and of the Opposition, a concept he largely developed during the politically chaotic 1850s. During 1852 alone he spoke on seventy-eight occasions in the House. Out of government there were fewer speeches but rarely less than fifty per year. His rhetorical skills were valuable to the Party, especially when so many of his colleagues lacked lustre.[11]

70

Budget, 1852

Hansard's Parliamentary Debates, Third Series, Vol.
123 (1853), cols. 836–8

24 x 28.5 cm

Parl. Deb. Eng. 225

Disraeli served as Chancellor of the Exchequer in
the short-lived 1852 'Who? Who? Ministry', so-
called after Wellington, very deaf, repeatedly
asked the Prime Minister, Lord Derby, to identify
the new Ministers as they spoke in the House of
Lords. The Cabinet's inexperience and commen-
tators' expectations have prompted comparisons
with the 1924 Labour Government,[12] but
Disraeli's appointment as Chancellor rather than
Foreign Secretary, to minimize contact with a
monarch sceptical about his integrity, also links it
to that of 1945 and the appointment of Hugh
(later Baron) Dalton (1887–1962) as Chancellor
rather than Foreign Secretary.

This extract is from Disraeli's s five-hour Budget
speech on 3 December 1852, which fills forty-two
pages in *Hansard*. Disraeli had worked assiduously
on his taxation proposals and estimates, but had
to revise the latter at the last minute to accommodate larger figures for the Navy. Earlier difficulties
with his own party over protection were compounded by Gladstone's intervention in the
closing stages of the debate. Gladstone queried
the non-existent surplus and stressed Disraeli's
ministerial inexperience. The heated exchanges
opened a rift which subsequent events
intensified. References in column 838 to
harmonizing financial and commercial policy,
and the pressures on agriculture, show Disraeli
still obliged to accommodate the Protectionists.
The Budget marked Disraeli's return to the
party's mainstream, but the immediate
consequence was the government's defeat and
resignation. (See Kenneth Clarke, 'Disraeli as
Chancellor', pp. 13-15.)

837   *Supply—*   {Dec. 3, 1852}   *The Budget.*   838

still I trust that hon. Members will have the kindness to recollect that it is a financial statement which has to be made under very peculiar circumstances; and, Sir, although we have, with respect to our finances, to consider to-night some very important topics—whether, for example, it is possible to make such changes in the mode of levying our revenue as may contribute more to the satisfaction and welfare of the community; whether such alterations can be effected in our method of taxation as may remove from various classes not an ill-founded sense of injury and injustice; and, still, whether we may not take this opportunity of establishing our financial system upon principles more adapted to the requirements of the times, and especially to the industry of a country pre-eminent for its capacity for labour—still, besides these, there are other topics to which I must advert, and which are not strictly of a financial nature. I hope the House will also remember that, even considering the remarks I have to offer to their consideration merely in a financial point of view, we are at the present moment we are only arrived at the completion of about two-thirds of the financial year—a circumstance which naturally adds to the difficulty I have to contend with. I hope, therefore, that under these circumstances hon. Members will not think it any evidence of conceit or affectation on my part if I do not on this occasion rigidly follow that routine form of exposition which a Chancellor of the Exchequer usually adopts at the termination or commencement of a financial year, when his duties are comparatively limited, and, I may say, comparatively simple; but, if I deviate from that course, I trust that they will attribute my proceeding to no other motive but a desire on my part, in dealing with these various important, and, in some cases, complicated subjects, to explain clearly to the House the views of Her Majesty's Government upon subjects of such great importance, and, so far as I have to touch upon the point, their opinion on the condition of the country. Sir, the task I have undertaken is, as the House is well aware, not a light one under any circumstances, and even under ordinary circumstances requires an appeal to the indulgence of the House. I am sure to-night I shall receive its generous indulgence; and the only favour I presume to ask of hon. Gentlemen on either side is, that they will not precipitately decide on any proposition which I

may make, but will consider all that I offer as a whole, because as a whole it ought to be considered; and I trust that, in justice to myself, they will not, until the views of the Government are fairly placed before them, be carried away by any feeling of the moment, on whichever side they may sit, too precipitately to decide on the motives and principles of the policy which I may now have to set before them.

Sir, we wished after the event of the last general election, understanding as we did from the result of that election that the principle of unrestricted competition was entirely and finally adopted as the principle of our commercial code—we wished to consider our financial system in relation to our commercial system—to see whether they could not be brought more in harmony together, and whether, in bringing them more in harmony together, we might not remove many well-founded causes of discontent among the people of this country, and lay the foundation of a system which in future should not only be more beneficial, but which should enlist in its favour the sympathies of all classes. Before, however, I take that general view, I think it will be convenient that I should consider the claims of those who believe that by what we now familiarly describe as "recent legislation" they have received peculiar injury. It will, I think, be for the convenience of the House that we should dispassionately consider the position of those classes, and come to an opinion whether their complaints and claims are just or not—because, if we can arrive at some conclusions on these points, those classes who now assert that they have been injured by recent legislation, if their claims are impartially heard, and, if established, fairly met, will then merge in the mass of the community, and we shall hereafter have to consider no other claims than claims which represent the unanimous voice and feeling of the entire nation. Therefore, I repeat, it will not be an inconvenient course if I take the earliest opportunity of examining the claims urged by those great interests which have been peculiarly affected by recent changes in our commercial law—the shipping interest for example, the sugar-producing interest, and the agricultural interest—so far as the latter, irrespective of all other pleas, urges on the consideration of the House the fact that it is subjected to peculiar burdens and taxation. When we have discussed

2 E 2

71
The Chancellor of the Exchequer's robe and Downing Street furniture

(The Chancellor's official residence, now No. 11, was then No. 12)

18.3 x 11.5; 18.3 x 23 cm

Dep. Hughenden 129/1, fols. 18–19

In the early months of 1853 Disraeli and Gladstone locked horns over possession of the Chancellor's robe and furniture. Disraeli, the loser in their Budget clash and financially stretched without his £5,000 ministerial salary (his debts would shortly exceed £25,000) insisted on payment for the furniture which he'd had to buy from his predecessor. He had only been partly reimbursed by the Office of Works and wanted Gladstone to pay the difference of £307. Disraeli also refused to relinquish the historic robes which were traditionally passed down to each succeeding holder of the post. They were possibly first worn by William Pitt (1759–1806).

Gladstone opens this letter written in January 1853 with 'My Dear Sir', and explains the reasons for delay. Soon they were both using the third person. Ultimately Gladstone, not the Office of Works, paid for the furniture and he ordered a new set of robes which Sir William Harcourt (1827–1904) retained when he left the office in 1895.

72
The Chancellor's robe
Reproduced by permission of Hughenden Manor
(The National Trust).
Black silk damask with gold braid
Recently restored robe on display at Hughenden
Manor

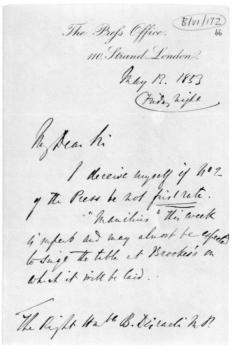

73
Disraeli and *The Press*
17.7 x 11.3 cm
Dep. Hughenden 37/3, fols. 66–7

Many of the key stepping stones in this stage of
Disraeli's life are located within the confines of
the Palace of Westminster and Whitehall's
corridors but he also channelled his energies into
establishing a weekly newspaper, *The Press*, as a
vehicle for progressive Conservatism which might
appeal to disaffected moderate Whigs.

The first issue of *The Press* appeared on 7 May
1853. It was edited by Samuel Lucas (1818–68), a
lawyer by training and regular contributor to *The
Times,* who Disraeli recruited. Disraeli was a
frequent but anonymous (and sometimes vitriolic)
contributor. The newspaper also carried items by
several of his long-standing friends including

Bulwer Lytton, the 'Manilus' referred to by Lucas
in the letter here, George Smythe, and Lord
Stanley, another of those whose intellectually
stimulating company Disraeli valued.

Disraeli's anomalous position as both party leader
and owner of a mouthpiece for one wing ended
with the return to office in 1858 and his sale of the
Press. The Press' second issue included an article
on Disraeli's Budget, a complementary piece on
Tea Duties and a 'striking' improvement in
coverage of 'general news – Art, Drama, Music…,
Literature'. [Brooke's refers to one of the leading
gentlemen's clubs.]

74

Return to Government, 1858

18 x 11 cm

Dep. Hughenden 109/2, fols. 159–60

Disraeli returned to office as Chancellor in Derby's second minority government of 1858–9. In the prevailing political climate, where coalition building was routine, the Conservatives tried to strengthen their leadership by enlisting heavyweights like Gladstone. In this letter written on the night of 21 February 1858, Lord Derby briefs Disraeli about the failure to recruit Gladstone (partly because Disraeli's overly-flattering letter backfired), which effectively ended the former's links with the Conservatives; and about the misgivings of his own son Stanley trying to form a government without a coalition partner (he later overcame these to join as Colonial Secretary). Overleaf Derby lists those who had accepted and records Queen Victoria's express wish that the 5th Duke of Richmond (1791–1860) should run the War Office. As Derby anticipated, Richmond refused.

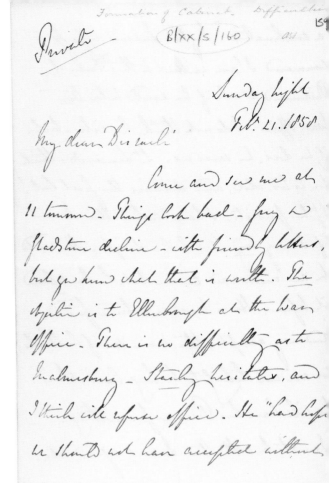

76

A political partnership

Glazed pottery mug 9 x10 cm [1850s]

Lent by a private collector

This small jug with black and white transfer portraits of Disraeli and Lord Derby may have been produced during the 1858–9 Conservative Government.

75

The Munificent Mrs Brydges Willyams

MS. Eng. lett. d. 341, fols. 86–7

Among the Bodleian Library's collections relating to Disraeli are three volumes of typewritten copies of the correspondence of Disraeli and his wife with Mrs Brydges Wylliams (d. 1863) which were previously in E. L. de Rothschild's library. The editors of the Disraeli project calculate that Mrs Brydges Willyams ranks third (after Lord Derby and his son Lord Stanley) as the recipient of the largest number of letters from Disraeli in the 1850s.

Mrs Sarah Brydges Willyams was a wealthy octogenarian widow who claimed to be distantly connected to Disraeli. She befriended him in 1851, made him her executor and a legatee (he eventually inherited about £30,000) and left instructions about her burial at Hughenden. The Disraelis visited her annually at Torquay. In the second half

of the 1850s Disraeli wrote over 30 letters a year to her. Like the Liberal Prime Minister, H. H. Asquith, Earl of Oxford and Asquith (1852–1928), many of his most descriptive letters were written to women, though the parallel is not exact.

This letter written from Downing Street on 16 June 1858 gives a lively account of Disraeli's heavy workload, Derby's health and the likely strains upon it, and Lord Stanley's indispensability. His ironic comparison between his political enemies and the Sepoys in the recent early Indian independence battles between guerrilla forces led by Tatya Tope and the British under Sir Colin (later Baron) Campbell (1792–1863) jars with today's sensibilities, though the tone conceals the seriousness with which he viewed his responsibilities.

86

Downing Street
June 16, 1858.

It is a long time since I said to you how d'ye do?

My life has been passed in constant combat, but I am glad to add with respect to all important matters, constant victory. The enemy, however, like the Sepoys, still keep the field, and, like Sir Colin, I really have to carry on the campaign under a scorching sky. Morning sittings, and evening sittings, with the duties of my Department, Cabinet Councils, and the general conduct of affairs, engross and absorb my life, from the moment I wake until the hour of rest, which is generally three hours after midnight.

But I never was better. I am sorry to say I cannot aver as much of my chief and colleague. Lord Derby has a raging fit of the gout, which terribly disconcerts me. Fortunately, we are now, generally speaking, on velvet; but unhappily, all the measures which I have carried through the House of Commons will soon be going to the Upper House, and he will be required to advocate and conduct them.

Our settlement of the Neapolitan difficulties has gained us great credit, and I hear from all parts of the country, that the Government is not only popular, but daily increasing in public favour. Lord Stanley is of great use to me, and much distinguishes himself.

I went in for five minutes the other day, to a morning party at Lady Londonderry's, and there I saw your

87

friend, Lady Brownlow, who gave me news of you. I wished to have called on her, but I have never had a moment to myself.

Your beautiful bay must be looking like Naples. I have never been in the country for five months except a little visit to Windsor = even when I went to Slough, the famous Slough, it was with a return ticket. But with success one can bear anything.

Yours ever,

D.

77
Queen Victoria (1819–1901) by G. Koberwein,
after von Angeli, 1876.
Oil on canvas, 91 x 76.2 cm, reproduced by
permission of Hughenden Manor (The National
Trust). The original was presented by the Queen
to Disraeli in 1876.

78
Edward Henry Stanley, 15ᵗʰ Earl of Derby
(1826–93), by Jane Hawkins after Sir Francis
Grant, PRA, n.d.
Oil on canvas, 94 x 84 cm, reproduced by
permission of Hughenden Manor (The National
Trust).

80

Montagu Corry, Lord Rowton (1838–1903)
Cartoon by *Spy* (Sir Leslie Ward, 1851–1922),
Power of Place [n.d.], 39.4 x 27.1 cm, reproduced by
permission of Hughenden Manor (The National
Trust).

79

William Ewart Gladstone (1809–98)
Photograph, 1858, 30.5 x 22.5 cm, in Sir Arthur
Hallam, *A Few Years of the Life of Mary Elizabeth
Elton* (privately printed at Clevedon Court, 1877).
211 C.17

82
Disraeli's Cabinet, [1877?]
Engraving, 74 x 101 cm, reproduced by permission
of Philip Waller, Merton College, Oxford.
Letters from Northcote (seated front left) the 15th
Earl of Derby (seated second left), Lord John
Manners (standing to the left of Disraeli) and
Salisbury (standing front right of picture) are
among those published in this book.

81
Sir Stafford Northcote, Lord Iddesleigh
(1818–87)
Photograph in Cornelius Brown (ed.), *An*
appreciative life of the Rt. Hon. The Earl of
Beaconsfield (London, 1881).
210 h.346

83
Robert Gascoyne-Cecil, 3ʳᵈ Marquess of Salisbury (1830–1903) wearing his robes as Chancellor of the University of Oxford.
Oil on canvas, 88.8 x 78.7 cm, reproduced by permission of Hughenden Manor (The National Trust).

84
Mary, Countess of Derby, by J.R. Swinton
Oil on canvas, 91 x 81.3 cm, reproduced by permission of Hughenden Manor (The National Trust).

85
Selina, Countess of Bradford, by G. Clarke,
after Sir Francis Grant, PRA.
Oil on canvas, 58.4 x 48.3 cm, reproduced by
permission of Hughenden Manor (The National
Trust).

86
Anne, Countess of Chesterfield, by F. P.
Graves, 1874, after Landseer
Oil on panel, 58.5 x 47 cm, reproduced by
permission of Hughenden Manor (The National
Trust).

87
Photograph, 12 x 17.5 cm, by the well-known
Oxford photographer H. W. Taunt
showing **Disraeli** with (clockwise) **Lord
Pembroke, Lady Bradford, Montagu Corry,
Lord Bradford, Lord Wharncliffe** and **Lady
Wharncliffe** at Hughenden, Whitsun 1874.
Reproduced by permission of the John Murray
Archive.

88
Thomas Norton Longman V
16.5 x 12.3 cm monochrome half-tone reproduc-
tion of original oil painting
On loan from Annabel Jones

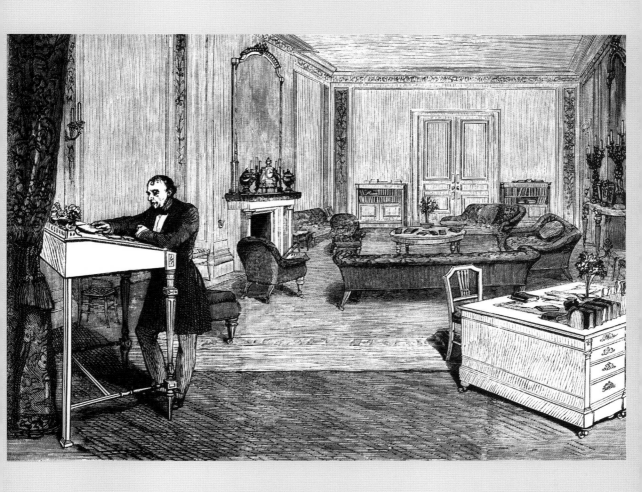

89

Disraeli at home in 19 Curzon Street

18.5 x 26.2 cm

Illustration in G.B. Smith, *The Life of the Rt. Hon.*
W. E. Gladstone, Vol. VI (1883), p. 325.

210 h.338

90

The reading desk

The desk, 130 cm at its highest point, and made of
satinwood inlaid with red velvet, is now at
Hughenden Manor.

CHAPTER SEVEN

1859–67

First Step, then 'Leap into the Dark'

Electoral Reform

POPULAR DEMAND for electoral reform provided Disraeli with opportunities for re-establishing the Conservatives as a national party, a majority government. The 'leap into the dark' – a phrase taken by Lord Cranborne (later 3rd Marquess of Salisbury) from the dying words of the seventeenth-century philosopher Thomas Hobbes, led to the Conservatives successfully introducing household (male) suffrage, effectively outdoing the Liberals in radicalism.

The Right Honourable B Disraeli 1867
from a portrait in the possession of
Major Coningsby Disraeli

92
Disraeli in 1867
Engraving, 21 x 13 cm, in Monypenny & Buckle, *The Life of Benjamin Disraeli*, Vol. IV (London, 1916). Reproduced by permission of John Murray Publishers. The portrait was formerly owned by Disraeli's nephew, Major Coningsby Disraeli
2288 e. 689/4

in lands or tenements of freehold tenure, of the clear yearly value over and above all charges and incumbrances affecting the same, of not less than *forty shillings*;

Copyholds of Inheritance. 2. Or shall be so beneficially entitled to an estate of inheritance in lands or tenements of copyhold, or any other tenure whatever, except freehold, of such clear yearly value, as aforesaid, of not less than *five pounds*;

Estates for lives. 3. Or shall be so beneficially entitled to an estate for any life or lives in lands or tenements, of any tenure, of such clear yearly value, as aforesaid, of not less than *five pounds*;

For years. 4. Or shall be so beneficially entitled to a term originally granted for not less than thirty years in lands or tenements, of any tenure, of such clear yearly value, as aforesaid, of not less than *five pounds*;

Tenant Occupiers. 5. Or shall occupy as tenant any such lands or tenements of the clear yearly value of not less than *ten pounds*;

Lodgers. 6. Or shall occupy any apartments in, or portion of a house, whether furnished or unfurnished, for which he shall have paid a rent of not less than *eight shillings* per week, or per annum, to an amount of *twenty pounds*;

Annual income from personal property. 7. Or shall be in the beneficial enjoyment of a yearly income arising from the personal property following, that is to say: From any annuity granted by the Commissioners for Reduction of the National Debt, or any dividends or interest from the Parliamentary stocks or funds of the United Kingdom, or from the stocks, shares, or bonds, of the East India Company, or of the Bank of England, standing in his own name, of not less amount per annum than *ten pounds*;

Income from Pensions, Superannuations, &c. 8. Or shall be in the beneficial enjoyment of an income arising from any pension, pay, or superannuation allowance, in respect of any past employment by such person in any department of Her Majesty's naval, military, East Indian or civil service, and who shall no longer be permanently employed therein, amounting to not less per annum than *twenty pounds*;

9. Or

Savings bank deposit. 9. Or shall hold, and shall be beneficially entitled to a deposit in some Savings Bank, established in England or Wales, under the provisions of the Act of the the ninth year of his late Majesty King George the 4th, cap. 92, to the amount of *sixty pounds*;

Educational qualifications. 10. Or shall possess one or other of the qualifications following, that is to say:—

Graduates. Who shall be a graduate of any University of the United Kingdom.

Clergy of Church of England. Or an ordained priest or deacon of the Church of England;

Other ministers. Or a minister of any other religious denomination appointed either alone or with not more than one colleague, to the charge of any chapel or place of worship, and officiating as the minister thereof;

Barristers, &c. Or a barrister-at-law, or serjeant-at-law, in any of the Inns of Court in England, or a certificated pleader or conveyancer;

Attorneys and solicitors. Or a certificated attorney, or solicitor, or proctor in England and Wales;

Medical profession. Or a member of the medical profession, registered under the provisions of "The Medical Act," 1858;

Middle Class Degrees. Or an associate in arts of any University of the United Kingdom;

Certificated Schoolmasters. Or a schoolmaster, holding a certificate from the Committee of Her Majesty's Council on Education.

Reserving rights of freemen, &c. 11. Or who shall be entitled to be registered for any county, city, or borough, in respect of any estate for life in freehold lands or tenements, of which he shall be seized at the time of the passing of this Act, or in respect of any qualification, as freeholder, burgage tenant, burgess, freeman, liveryman, or otherwise, reserved or defined in the 31st, 32nd, 33rd, 34th, and 35th sections of the Act of the second year of the reign of His late Majesty King William IV, cap. 45.

Possession for a certain time, and registration essential to right of voting. II. No person shall be entitled to vote, as aforesaid, unless he shall have been duly registered according to the provisions hereinafter contained;

B

91
Strategies & 'Fancy Franchises'

34.5 x 42 cm draft Parliamentary Representation Bill, 1859
Dep. Hughenden 43/3, fols. 132–3

In March 1859 Disraeli introduced a Second Reform Bill to extend the franchise, fulfilling a pledge made by Lord Derby at the opening of the 1859 session.

Both the Conservatives and the future Liberal Governments (as they became known) responded to popular pressure for reform between 1852 and 1867, determined to gain electorally. The issue was internally divisive. An unenthusiastic Cabinet (two ministers resigned) agreed to extend the £10 householder franchise from the boroughs to the counties, added a new £20 lodger category in both and a number of 'fancy franchises'. The Conservatives would have benefited from a proposed redistribution of seats. These pages from the draft bill list some of the 'fancy franchises' – as the Radical John Bright (1811–89) termed them – which Disraeli is believed to have devised. The Bill was too partisan, and its defeat by the Liberals and Radicals brought down the Government.

93
'Hot on Reform'

18 x 11.4 cm
Dep. Hughenden 110/3, fol. 17

The Conservatives returned to power as a
minority government in the summer of 1866.
With Liberal plans for electoral reform derailed
by the Conservatives combining with the
'Adullamite' Liberal opponents, the Conservatives
were ready to exploit the situation. As Derby
observes in this brief note of 6 February 1867 to
Disraeli, again Chancellor of the Exchequer, the
new parliamentary session had opened well 'but
they are very hot on reform <u>without delay</u>'.
Disraeli's use of electoral reform to disadvantage
the Liberals has been compared to another
opportunist David (later 1st Earl), Lloyd George
(1863–1945).[13] More recently his behaviour in 1867
has been likened to a 'basketful of eels'.[14] His
opportunism combining with the political courage
for which he was famous and his willingness to
use reform to protect the 'aristocratic settlement'
to which he was committed.

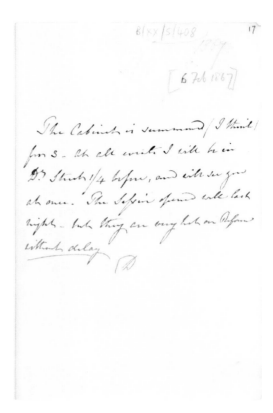

94
Ministerial casualties

23.5 x 37.5 cm
Dep. Hughenden 92/1, fols. 39v–40r

Intent on 'extricat[ing]' themselves from the
'Reform Dilemma' by the 'extension to Household
suffrage', Derby and Disraeli encountered
opposition within the Cabinet.[15] Lord Cranborne,
the future Marquess of Salisbury (1830–1903) who
would serve under Disraeli as Foreign Secretary,
was one of those strongly opposed to widening
the franchise. He doubted the viability of
'neutralizing' safeguards such as multiple votes for
property owners. Having helped to defeat Lord
John Russell's bill he marshalled statistics to
counter his own party's plans. On 25 February
Disraeli's attempt to commit the Government to

legislation without Cabinet support led to 'the
Ten minute bill' (so-called because of last-minute
agreement) and scenes of high drama before its
withdrawal. Cranborne, outlining his concerns
about borough franchises to Disraeli in this letter
of 1 February, was unpersuaded, and resigned as
Secretary of State for India with Lord Carnarvon
(1831–90) and Peel's younger brother, General Peel
(1799–1879) on 2 March, a move likened by Roy
Jenkins to Enoch Powell's resignation with Nigel
Birch and Peter Thorneycroft from the
Macmillan government in 1958.[16]

95
Lord Cranborne's resignation

17.7 x 11.2; 17.7 x 11.2 cm

Dep. Hughenden 92/1, fol. 45$^{r \& v}$

Disraeli pressed on, defeating Gladstonian amendments en route. The Bill which eventually passed into law in August 1867 enfranchised roughly a million male voters, more than double the number originally envisaged – and without any inbuilt safeguards. The Conservatives had stolen the march by 'Dishing the Whigs'. In debate Cranborne spoke about the baleful affects of political adventurers but Disraeli's gamble – or intuition – paid off. The newly enfranchised working class in the boroughs became key Conservative voters.

96
'The Political Egg-Dance'

Cartoon No. 55 in *The Earl of Beaconsfield KG Cartoons from "Punch", 1843–1878* (London, 1878).
29 x 22 cm

Punch's comment on Disraeli's management of the Reform Bill in the House of Commons.
Johnson d. 4932

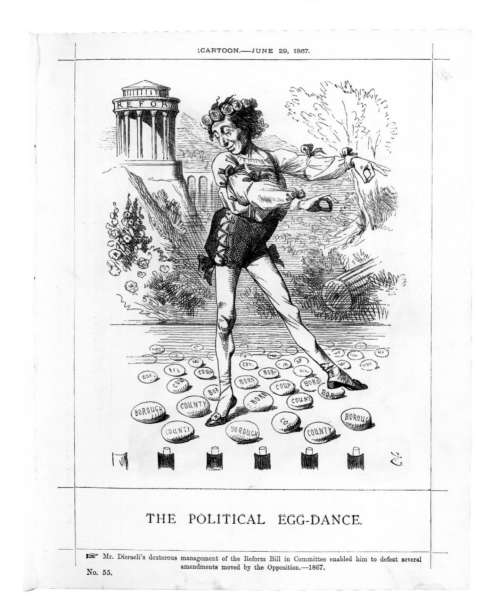

CARTOON.—JUNE 29, 1867.

THE POLITICAL EGG-DANCE.

☞ Mr. Disraeli's dexterous management of the Reform Bill in Committee enabled him to defeat several
amendments moved by the Opposition.—1867.

No. 55.

97
'Too much overlooked'

20.5 x 12.8; 41 x 25.6; 20.5 x 12.8 cm
Dep. Hughenden 40/1, fols. 115–16, 117

Women were still denied the vote (though
Disraeli was personally not hostile to enfranchis-
ing those with property). Between March 1867
and June 1868 the Lancashire Committee for the
Enfranchisement of Women/Manchester
National Society for Women's Suffrage put their
case before Disraeli in four letters. Here Lydia
Becker, the Hon. Secretary, writes in March 1867
about those whose claim had been 'too much
overlooked', women like the Manchester '...school
mistresses, yarn agents, bleachers, calico printers
and shopkeepers [who] contribute by their
industry and energy to the wealth of the city and
the prosperity of the country'.

Lancashire Committee for the
ENFRANCHISEMENT OF WOMEN.

10, Grove-street, Ardwick, Manchester.
March 2. 1867.

98
Reform Agenda
72.5 x 57.5 cm Decorated Address (roll)
Dep. Hughenden 371/1

In October 1867 upwards of 2,500 signatories contributed to the Address presented to Disraeli by the Working men of Edinburgh. Alongside praise for his skills in securing for his 'humbler countrymen the privileges of citizenship' are calls for extending the reform to Scotland, finding a solution to the Irish question, support for trades unions, and for national education programmes for both school children and adults.

99
Reform Mapped
'Stanford's guide map [ca.1:1,650,000] to the constituencies of England & Wales, Ireland & Scotland shewing all the counties, divisions of counties parliamentary boroughs & universities with the alterations & additions according to the "Representation of the People Acts, 1867–8" and the number of members for each constituency'
London: Edward Stanford, 6. & 7. Charing Cross, 1868.
30.25 x 22.25 cm
C15 (182)

This map published in 1868 is the earliest example of British General Election mapping held in the Bodleian Library. Stanford's was established in 1852 by map seller Edward Stanford. Alive to the impact that the expansion of British colonialism and the increase in overseas travel would have on his business, Stanford exploited his position as the only map seller in London, taking over 7 and 8 Charing Cross and acquiring premises in Trinity Place for use as a printing works.

Stanfords produced later versions showing the political make-up of the British Isles 'according to the Redistribution of Seats Act 1885'. Stanford's election maps remain a feature of the political scene; their latest version was published in 2001.

CHAPTER EIGHT

1868–72

Political Gain, Literary Success and Personal Loss

Leader of the Party and Permier, 1868

As a PARLIAMENTARIAN, and as a minister, Disraeli worked prodigiously. As Leader of the Party in the Commons and effectively Leader of the Opposition from 1849 he had immersed himself in dispatches and government Blue Books. This was partly because of the insecurity of his position within the party but also because politics mattered to him. His mastery of the throwaway line might suggest it was a great game, but underneath the surface there was a more serious intent. By the time he became Prime Minister the struggle to the top had sapped his energies – as he would later say, power had come too late. He still believed in his destiny to lead, but after the party's defeat in the 1868 election there were many who thought otherwise.

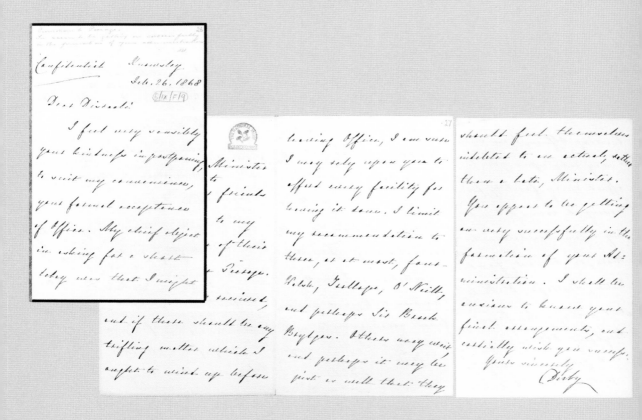

one – Hunt, I think, would do his work well, and if you think Walpole would not do I think you had better take him. I am quite sure you ought not to attempt to combine the offices of First Lord & the Exchequer, unless it were as a temporary arrangement –

with a view to a coalition of some kind; of which I see no prospect. If matters so turn as to make you wish me to go to the Exchequer I am quite ready; though I would much rather stay where I am, with all the work I now have in hand.

Yours very faithfully
Stafford H. Northcote –

101

Northcote advises

18.7 x 23.5 cm
Dep. Hughenden 41/1, fols. 48–9

In this letter from his home in Harley Street Sir Stafford Northcote, later Lord Iddesleigh (1818–87), Cranborne's successor at the India Office, a future Chancellor of the Exchequer and leader of the Conservatives in the Commons, suggests George Ward Hunt (1825–77) as Chancellor if Disraeli considered [Spencer] Walpole (1806–98) unacceptable (he retired), and advises against Disraeli trying to combine the Premiership with the Chancellorship. His comment about his own preferences could be read as a marker for the future. A very modern letter despite being written nearly 140 years ago. Northcote, acting as Disraeli's intermediary, invited Cranborne to rejoin the Cabinet but, unsurprisingly, was rebuffed.

100

Lord Derby departs

18.2 x 11.2; 18.2 x 22.4; 18.2 x 11.2 cm
Dep. Hughenden 41/1, fols. 26–7

In February 1868 an ailing Lord Derby resigned as Prime Minister and Leader of the Party. In this confidential letter written from Knowsley he thanked Disraeli for agreeing to postpone his formal acceptance of office for a few days until he, Derby, had drawn up the Victorian equivalent of the contemporary resignation honours list. He intended to nominate three, at most four: Welsh, Trollope, O'Neill and possibly Sir Brook Brydges, believing it wise to let other candidates depend on Disraeli for their elevation. The letter closed by praising Disraeli's choice of ministers and wishing him success. Derby had said that he would always be there for Disraeli if he needed to consult him, and this relationship lasted until Derby's death the following year.

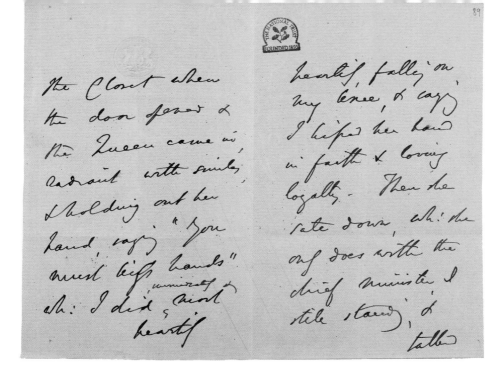

102

First Audience as Prime Minister

18 x 11.5 cm
Dep. Hughenden 41/1, fols. 88–9

Disraeli became Prime Minister on 27 February.
Here, in a confidential letter written from
Osborne the following day, Disraeli describes to
his private secretary, Montagu Corry, his first
audience with Queen Victoria as her Premier. He
arrived at 7 p.m.; about half an hour afterwards
the door opened, '& the Queen came in radiant
with smiles, holding out her hand, saying "You
must kiss hands…"' which he did 'most heartily'
falling on his knee 'saying [that] I kissed her hand
"in faith & loving loyalty"'. They talked so long he
hardly had time to dress for dinner, dining almost
'quite alone' with Princess Louise and the
Duchess of Athlone. This rapport would be
enhanced by his lively written reports. Corry, later
Lord Rowton (1838–1903), was another of those
aristocratic, agreeable young men (his maternal
grandfather was the 6th Lord Shaftesbury) with
whom Disraeli surrounded himself. He was
recruited by Disraeli to be his Private Secretary in
1866. Queen Victoria would later remark that
Corry had devoted himself to Disraeli 'as few sons
ever do'. In his last novel, *Endymion*, Disraeli

would describe the bond between a minister and
his secretary as among the finest that exist outside
'the married state'.

Disraeli had reached the top of the greasy-pole
but his position was not secure within his own
party. Moreover he was tired by the long climb.
Yet he was not a spent force. Out of government
from December 1868 he spent 1869 writing a
thriller, *Lothair*. Published in 1870, it ran to eight
English editions. Set again in 'the grand social
world' in which he been 'a slightly mocking
traveller for over thirty years', it has been
described as Wildean before Wilde.[17]

The interval between his two Premierships was
not without highlights – improvements in the
party organization with the creation of the
National Union of Constituency Associations in
1867, and his speeches in Manchester and at
Crystal Palace in 1872, but it was darkened by
Mary Anne's failing health.

103

'He lives on the Hope of a General Election'

Caricature of Disraeli in 19 July 1871 issue of *The Hornet*

39.5 x 26.8 cm

John Johnson Collection, Political General 1 (33)

Both Disraeli's mournful expression and the caption imply that like most politicians he preferred to be in the government rather than in the government in waiting.

THE HORNET.

WEDNESDAY.]   [JULY 19TH, 1871.

DIZZY.

He lives on the hope of a General Election.

10

their provisions, and it touches upon all the means by which you may wean them from habits of excess and of brutality. Now, what is the feeling upon these subjects of the Liberal party—that Liberal party who opposed the Tory party when, even in their weakness, they advocated a diminution of the toil of the people, and introduced and supported those Factory Laws, the principles of which they extended, in the brief period when they possessed power, to every other trade in the country? What is the opinion of the great Liberal party—the party that seeks to substitute cosmopolitan for national principles in the government of this country—on this subject? Why, the views which I expressed in the great capital of the county of Lancaster have been held up to derision by the Liberal Press. A leading member—a very rising member, at least, among the new Liberal members—denounced them the other day as the "policy of sewage." Well, it may be the "policy of sewage" to a Liberal member of Parliament. But to one of the labouring multitude of England, who has found fever always to be one of the inmates of his household—who has, year after year, seen stricken down the children of his loins, on whose sympathy and material support he has looked with hope and confidence, it is not a "policy of sewage," but a question of life and death. And I can tell you this, gentlemen, from personal conversation with some of the most intelligent of the labouring class—and I think there are many of them in this room who can bear witness to what I say—that the policy of the Tory party—the hereditary, the traditionary policy of the Tory party, that would improve the condition of the people—is more appreciated by the people than the ineffable mysteries and all the pains and penalties of the Ballot Bill. Gentlemen, is that wonderful? Consider the condition of the great body of the working classes of this country. They are in possession of personal privileges—of personal rights and liberties—which are not enjoyed by the aristocracies of other countries. Recently they have obtained—and wisely obtained—a great extension of political rights; and when the people of England see that under the constitution of this country, by means of the constitutional cause which my right hon. friend the Lord Mayor has proposed, they possess every personal right of freedom, and, according to the conviction of the whole country, also an adequate concession of political rights, is it at all wonderful that they should wish to elevate and improve their condition, and is it unreasonable that they should ask the Legislature to assist them in that behest as far as it is consistent with the general welfare of the realm? Why, the people of England would be greater idiots than the Jacobinical leaders of London even suppose, if, with their experience and acuteness, they should not long have seen that the time had arrived when social, and not political improvement is the object which they ought to pursue. I have touched, gentlemen, on the three great objects of the Tory party. I told you I would try to ascertain what was the position of the Tory party with reference to the country now. I have

104

Crystal Palace Speech

21.3 x 27.5 cm printed pamphlet, 1872

Dep. Hughenden 66, item 17, p. 10

During the Crystal Palace speech on 24 June Disraeli outlined his tenets of conservatism: 'to maintain institutions, to uphold empire & to elevate the condition of the people'. Lord Morley (1838–1923), Gladstone's colleague and biographer, later wrote that with his 'rare faculty of wide and sweeping forecast' Disraeli had accurately read the 'characteristics of the time'.[18] The speech foreshadowed the social legislation which his government would introduce in 1875–6. It is regarded as one of Disraeli's defining contributions to the notion of progressive conservatism.

105

Death of Mary Anne, 1872

18 x 11.4; 18 x 22.8 cm

Dep. Hughenden 95/2, fols. 265–6

Mary Anne had attended the Manchester speech,
but advancing cancer made it one of her last
public appearances. In this letter written on 5
December 1872 Disraeli describes to Corry the
closing stages of her illness. Overwhelmed,
Disraeli was unable to apply his mind to political
matters.

106

The Queen's concern

21.2 x 27.4 cm

Dep. Hughenden 202/1, fol. 133

The Queen sent a total of six telegrams between
11 and 20 December, in the mornings, asking for
news of the Mary Anne's condition, and after her
death asked one of her Ladies-in-Waiting to
write to Disraeli requesting an account of his
wife's last hours. The Queen had wished to visit
Hughenden on her way to Osborne, but she had
been advised that her own cold and the distance
made it unwise. The fact that both Victoria and
Disraeli had lost their spouses would be another
factor in their working relationship in Disraeli's
last government.

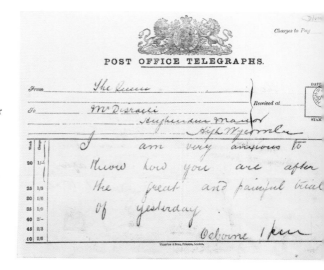

107

Loss

18 x 11.4; 18 x 22.8 cm

MS. Harcourt dep. 204, fols. 16–17

Among the large number of letters of condolence
Disraeli received was one from Sir William
Harcourt written on 3 January 1873. In this
acknowledgement Disraeli describes the loss of
his 'inseparable, & ever interesting companion'.
The story of how the gift of a case of Trinity
College, Cambridge, ale crossed party boundaries
(Harcourt, a Trinity man, would shortly join the
Liberal Cabinet) and comforted the dying wife of
the Conservative Leader is another thread linking
Disraeli to the Harcourts. In the twentieth
century Sir William's son, Lewis, later Lord
Harcourt (1863–1922) would recall the occasion
when he had accompanied his father to meet
Disraeli.

CHAPTER NINE

1874–80

The Final Summit

IN FEBRUARY 1874 the Conservatives were returned with a majority of over one hundred seats. Declining energy, personal preference and prime ministerial instincts led Disraeli to concentrate on foreign policy issues. A willingness to delegate ensured that his Government met its electoral pledges by introducing several key pieces of domestic reform, including the Trades Union, Public Health, Artisans Dwellings and Factory Acts. Collectively the reforms amounted to the largest tranche of social legislation passed by a nineteenth-century government.

Although a century of politics and party allegiance separates them, Disraeli's style of cabinet government is not unlike that of Clement (later Earl) Attlee (1883–1967) and James (later Lord) Callaghan (b. 1916). All three were pragmatic. Each was his own man, Lord Callaghan 'a cat that walked by himself'.[19] His wish to be Attlee-like and delegate the detail to others (an intention Disraeli would have understood) was soon overtaken by events. Lord Callaghan's predecessor as Prime Minister, Harold (later Lord) Wilson (1917–95), included Disraeli in his 1977 television programme *A Prime Minister on Prime Ministers*. As the draft script (see No. 139) reveals, Wilson was alive to Disraeli's shortcomings but nevertheless suggested that Disraeli '... stands so high among Britain's Prime Ministers regardless of policy [because] he had the personal vision, and the skill to create a vision for his country, his Queen, and his people'.

Disraeli's purchase of the Suez Canal and his response to the Eastern Question were part of larger party political and foreign policy strategies. His Palmerstonian stance attracted the newly-enfranchised voters, consolidating the Conservatives' identity as a national party. Over thirty years earlier he had agreed with the Newcastle Radical Charles Attwood 'an union between the Conservative party and Radical Masses offers the only means by which we can preserve the Empire....United they form the nation'.[20] But now his emphasis on the British Empire was a response to the beginning of the decline in British power in the 1870s. In containing Russia and protecting trade routes to India he was pursuing traditional British objectives. His policies confirmed Britain as an 'Asiatic' power rather than a European one; the *Dreikaiserbund,* the alliance of three Emperors (German, Austro-Hungarian and Russian) left little scope for the latter.[21]

The smouldering antagonism between Disraeli and Gladstone ignited again over the Eastern Question. Their clashes were not just about differences in political style and personality but conflicting visions for Britain's future.

108

Her Majesty's Invitation

17.5 x 11.3 cm

Dep. Hughenden 78/1, fols. 5–6

Following the Liberal defeat in the 1874 election Gladstone hesitated over whether the Government should resign immediately or fall back on precedent and wait until defeated in Parliament. The Queen favoured a quick resolution. Here she conveys news of the resignation of Gladstone and his colleagues, invites Disraeli to form a new government and sets the time for their meeting. These few words ushered in Disraeli's last Government. It had a solid parliamentary base but like his Labour successor as Prime Minister a century later in 1974, Harold Wilson, he was losing his zest for governing.

109

The Empress of India

17.7 x 23 cm

MS. Harcourt dep. 86, fols. 159–60

One of the best-known events in Disraeli's relationship with his 'Faery Queen', a term ironically borrowed from Spenser, is the controversial creation of the title 'Empress of India'. This August 1899 letter from Lord James of Hereford (1828–1911) to his former colleague, Sir William Harcourt, attributes the origins of the title to Disraeli and the 1858 Government of India Bill. They had thought 'Dizzy was the designer of the title' but then the Queen was known to style herself Empress of India in the 1860s. James now had documentary proof that it was Disraeli, although he had had to wait until he had a majority government to carry the measure.

110

European alliances

17.7 x 11.4 cm

Dep. Hughenden 78/3, fols. 227–8

In May 1875, with Germany seemingly on the verge of attacking France, Disraeli wanted to join the Russian protest. Intent on being more proactive than Gladstone and inspired by Palmerston's policy, Disraeli envisaged new European configurations possibly involving an alliance with Russia to maintain peace. Here Victoria asks for details of his conversation with the Russian Ambassador, Count Shouvaloff, seeks prompt advice on what to write to the Empress of Russia and wonders whether to write also to the Empress of Germany. When relations between Britain and Russia later deteriorated over the latter's designs on Turkey's European empire, Victoria's Russophobia compounded Disraeli's difficulties.

111

The Suez Canal

18.4 x 21.7 cm

Dep. Hughenden 106/3, fols. 74–6

In this letter written in November 1875 one of Disraeli's Young England protégés, Lord John Manners, by then Postmaster General, describes how de Lesseps viewed Britain's purchase of nearly half (44 per cent) of the Suez Canal Company shares. Disraeli's interest in the company pre-dated his final Premiership. He moved quickly, first to exploit the opportunities presented by de Lesseps' financial difficulties and then forestall the purchase of the Khedive's shares by the French, overriding the objections of his Foreign Secretary and most of the Cabinet. Few acquisitions would symbolize the expansion and the contraction of British power so dramatically. Purchased with a loan of £4,000,000 from the Rothschilds, this economic and strategic link to the empire lopped several weeks off the journey time to India. By 1875 four-fifths of the traffic was British. Eighty years later, in 1956, it was the scene of the British debacle.

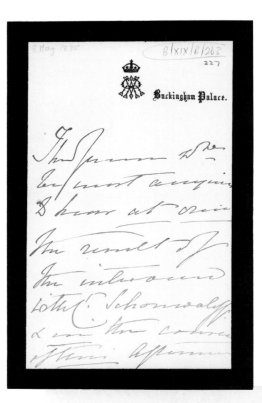

Oxford high Church party
might press upon him
the duty of not giving
way to Sir S. Northcote
I confess this possibility
had not struck me,
So I write it at once.
And this suggestion of
Stanley's raises another
reflection & doubt —
will the party consent

in the H. of L.
to have a leader chosen
for them? — Will it
not say the 'Liberals
as a party chose their
leader. we will choose
our's?
Would it be necessary
to say more to W. Hardy
tomorrow than that the
Queen had offered you
a Peerage & that you

should hold the Canal
than a poignée d'aventuriers
or intriguing states.'

I think I brought to your
notice in the summer the
name of Mr Page who
negociated and signed for
us at Berne the Postal
Union Treaty as a Candidate
for a Civil. C. B.
Canada and India have

112

Lady Derby counsels

18.4 x 22.8 cm
Dep. Hughenden 113/4, fols. 92–3

As 1876 progressed, ill health and murmurings
over his leadership of the Government prompted
Disraeli to consider resigning or moving to the
House of Lords: 'The Elysian Fields'. Derby
would have been his choice for Prime Minister
and Hardy leader of the party in the Commons
(Disraeli's role under Derby's father). But Derby
declined and Disraeli went to the Lords. Here
Lord Derby's wife, one of Disraeli's confidantes,
outlines her concerns about the succession and the
method of selection and adds that Lord Derby,
whom she refers to by his earlier title, was
unaware that she was writing to him.

NEUTRALITY UNDER DIFFICULTIES.

Dizzy. *"Bulgarian Atrocities! I can't find them in the 'Official Reports'!!!"*

☞ The country was deeply stirred by the dreadful outrages in Bulgaria, and Mr. Disraeli's attitude of official indifference called forth wide disapprobation.—1876.

No. 88.

113
Leaving for 'the Elsyian Fields'

Parliamentary Debates, Third Series, Vol. 231, cols.
1141–2
24.2 x 15 cm
Parl. Deb. Eng. 333

On 11 August 1876 Disraeli made his final
appearance in the House of Commons, during the
last debate of the session. His speech on the
Bulgarian atrocities runs to nine columns of
Hansard. The British Ambassador mentioned in
the opening minutes was the Turcophile Sir
Henry Elliot who, through a mixture of partisan-
ship and ill-health, had been reluctant to press
Turkey over the atrocities. Evidence for these was
now incontrovertible though the number of
casualties had been reduced from initial reports of
25,000 to 12,000. Disraeli spoke of the 'horrible
event which no one can think of without emotion'
(col. 1142) but then struck the wrong note by
refuting the argument that the losses amounted to
depopulating a whole province. He ended with a
pledge to defend the interests of the British
Empire but later acknowledged to Derby the
debate had damaged the Government.

114
'Neutrality under Difficulties'

Cartoon No. 88 in *The Earl of Beaconsfield KG
Cartoons from "Punch", 1843–1878* (London, 1878).
29 x 22 cm
Johnson d. 4932

Disraeli's response to news of the fate of the
Bulgarian Christians killed during the Turkish
suppression of their uprising brought opprobrium.
He believed that to acknowledge the deed would
strengthen Russian grounds for invading to
protect the Slav Christians, undermine the case
for defending Turkey's territorial integrity, and, as
he explained in a letter to Lady Chesterfield, risk
war in Europe. But his initial, flippant, comments,
are reminiscent of the youthful remarks made
during his Middle East tour, when he had
casually referred to the mass killings ordered by
the Bey. Disraeli didn't identify with the outrage
expressed over the atrocities and would describe
Gladstone's pamphlet on the Bulgarian atrocities
as (stylistically) the greatest atrocity.

115

'The Tables Turned'

Cartoon by G. Bridgman, [1876]
Printed on paper, 65 x 46.5 cm (including mount),
published by Reynolds & Co, 32 St James,
[London] S. W.
John Johnson Collection Gladstone folder 1 (52)

Gladstone's stand drew negative as well as positive comment. Here his support for the Christian Bulgarians provided a moral argument for Russia's action. The publication of his famous Bulgarian atrocities pamphlets in September 1876 drew on unsubstantiated reports in the press, vastly inflated the numbers of the victims in the gruesome events, and appeared to call for the expulsion of the Turks from Europe (later modified by Gladstone to refer to Turkish ministers). Disraeli was quick to comment on Gladstone's carelessness with the figures and the impact of his pamphlet on prospects of a settlement for a peaceful settlement (see above). Gladstone, reinvigorated, later returned to the leadership of the Liberals, and the premiership.

THE TABLES TURNED.
OR
WHO DANCES NOW?

137

116
'…Power and the Affections'

The Marquis of Zetland (ed.), *The Letters of Disraeli to Lady Bradford and Lady Chesterfield, 1876–1881*, Vol. II (London, 1929), p. 70
2288 d.381

Disraeli took Mary Anne at her word (when she encouraged him to remarry if she should die before him – see No. 129, below) and looked for a new partner. In 1873 he fell in love with the married Lady Bradford, the younger of the surviving daughters of Lord Forester, whom he had known since the 1830s. The extent to which his affection was reciprocated is unclear since most of her letters to Disraeli no longer survive – perhaps weeded out by Corry or Rose. In his letters to her, and to Lady Chesterfield, her widowed sister to whom he proposed, Disraeli vividly describes his daily life. Disraeli wrote roughly a thousand letters to Lady Bradford and half as many to her sister, prefiguring the highly descriptive letters H.H. Asquith wrote to the Stanley sisters forty years later. In this letter written in September 1876, he notes how the arrival of a letter from her '…generally rewards me and supports me for the whole day – but not always' and refers to his demanding schedule and the situation in the Balkans.

LETTERS OF DISRAELI

and by Russia's agents, though the Government have no more to do with the "atrocities" than the man in the moon. Gortchakoff is, of course, in the seventh heaven and smiles while he proposes an armistice of three months—equivalent to renewed war with renovated energies!

Think of me sometimes.

Yours ever,
B

On September 2nd the harassed Prime Minister gave Lady Bradford a graphic picture of the life which these tumultuous days imposed upon him:

Whatever happens I must write to you who remember me amid all your bustle and all the calls on your time and thought. But I can only repeat the bulletin of yesterday—aggravated; and so it will go on.

This is my life. I am called at 7—and my caller brings me my post—the Government bag and the outside letters, still very numerous. If I can get to my cabinet for work at 9 o'clock, I think myself content—and then I do a good deal. But at 11 the second post arrives—and all the newspapers which I must inspect, or at least glance at—and then my letters! It is the post that, if you write, brings one from you. It generally rewards me and supports me for the whole day—but not always. At one o'clock comes the daily messenger with all the boxes—and I have really to work immensely hard to get him off by half past 3, in time for the London post. It is absolutely necessary that I should have half an hour for luncheon, which is my real and almost only meal—on which I live.

It is hard to manage all this, but it is an exception when a telegram or two in cypher do not arrive about the same time—as they have done to-day. So pardon this—more than pardon it. I scarcely can write, and yet I should be unhappy if I did not. It is like building the walls of Jerusalem with a trowel in one hand and a sword in the other. I write quicker to you than "our own correspondent" at the seat of war, in the midst of a battle.

By the by, all the papers are arguing whether the great

70

117
Lord Salisbury's concerns
23.5 x 38.3 cm
Dep. Hughenden 92/4, fols. 3–6

Even before he became Foreign Secretary in 1878
Lord Salisbury was offering advice to Disraeli on
the conduct of policy. In this extract from a
closely argued eight-page letter written on 23
September 1876, he refers to the impact of the
Government's policy on the party's electoral
performance, the limits on British policy, and the
need to devise methods to protect the Christians
in the Turkish Empire. His suggestions included a
Minister of State nominated with the consent of
the signatories to the 1856 Treaty, who would be
involved in the selection of Governors of Bosnia,
Herzegovina and Bulgaria. Salisbury believed the
best way of resolving current 'perplexities' was 'to
come to an early understanding with Russia' and
distance themselves from the Austrian stance.

118
A friendship factured
19 x 12.3 cm
Dep. Hughenden 113/2, fols. 38–9

In April 1877 Russia went to war against Turkey.
Nine months later the Russians were closing in on
Constantinople. War fever swept Britain and the
term 'jingo' was coined. Disraeli and Derby
diverged over the means to avoid war. Disraeli was
willing to threaten force. Alarmed by the prospect
of war and close to breakdown, Derby had
resorted to the extraordinary device of leaking
cabinet discussions to Shouvaloff. Lady Derby did
likewise.

In this letter written on 23 January Derby explains
that he could not defend the decision to send the
fleet to Constantinople. At Disraeli's request he
postponed the announcement. A temporary recall
of the fleet undercut Derby's argument but he
finally left office on 27 March. After more than
thirty years of collaboration, spanning two
generations, the Disraeli–Derby link was broken.

119

Disraeli and Gladstone lock horns again

17.4 x 11.2; 17.4 x 22.4 cm; 22.5 x 36.8 cm

Dep. Hughenden 129/1, fols. 89–90 & 99–100

The antipathy between Disraeli and Gladstone resurfaced in the summer of 1878. Disraeli and Salisbury had returned from the Congress of Berlin (held to settle the Russo-Turkish war) as national heroes, having secured the reform of the Turkish Administration, acquiring Cyprus and 'Peace with Honour' – a term later fatefully used by Neville Chamberlain on his return from meeting Hitler in 1938. Disraeli was irritated by Gladstone describing the Cyprus acquisition as an 'act of duplicity'. In a speech in Knightsbridge a few days before this exchange of letters he'd famously characterized Gladstone as 'inebriated with the exuberance of his own verbosity… command[ing] interminable …series of arguments to malign an opponent and glorify himself'.[22] Disraeli complained in the House of Lords about the attacks on his character. Gladstone replied the following day in the Commons. These extracts give a flavour of their stances, Disraeli seeking to elevate his by referring to the pressing demands of office, but conceding that the term 'devilish' had been used by one of Gladstone's colleagues.

120

The '*Pas De Deux!*' of two Knights of the Garter, from the cartoon by Sir John Tenniel

29 x 22 cm

Cartoon No. 104 in *The Earl of Beaconsfield KG Cartoons from "Punch", 1843–1878* (1878)

Johnson d. 4932

Both Disraeli and Salisbury were admitted to the order of the Knights of the Garter, the highest order of British knighthood, in acknowledgment of their efforts at the Congress of Berlin. Disraeli made his acceptance conditional on Salisbury being awarded the honour, too. Twentieth-century prime-ministerial recipients include H.H. Asquith, Sir Winston Churchill, Clement Attlee, Harold Wilson and James Callaghan. Salisbury, once one of Disraeli's fiercest critics, would be 'fill[ed] with sadness and helplessness' when he heard news of Disraeli's death.[23]

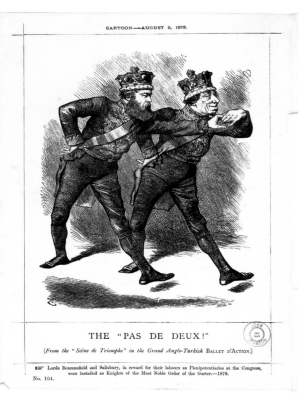

CARTOON—AUGUST 3, 1878.

THE "PAS DE DEUX!"

(From the "Scène de Triomphe" in the Grand Anglo-Turkish BALLET D'ACTION.)

Lords Beaconsfield and Salisbury, in reward for their labours as Plenipotentiaries at the Congress, were installed as Knights of the Most Noble Order of the Garter.—1878.

No. 104.

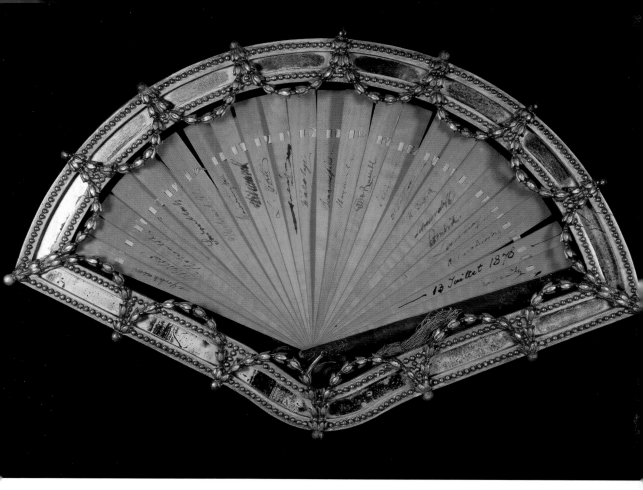

123

Dispatch box

17 high x 32.8 wide x 19.5 cm deep
Rectangular, covered with red-dyed, long-grain
morocco leather. The top is stamped
'Rᵀ. HON.ᴮᴸᴱ B. DISRAELI'.
Reproduced by permission of Hughenden Manor
(The National Trust).

121

Memento

35.5 x 55.9 cm
Cherrywood, gilt and mirror fan framed with beadings and swags.
Taken to the Congress of Berlin by Mahomet Ali, signed by all
members of the Congress and presented to Hughenden by Sir
Alexander R. Murray (1872–1957), who lived nearby.
Reproduced by permission of Hughenden
Manor (The National Trust).

122

Plate

23 cm
Fluted, glazed plate with
transfer print of Disraeli
[1880s]. Lent by a private
collector

CHAPTER TEN

1880–1

The Final Chapter

'Men with missions do not disappear till they have fulfilled them' (*Endymion*).

DISRAELI ACCEPTED DEFEAT at the hands of the electorate 'stoically' and perhaps with relief. Berlin had been exhausting; the situations in Africa and India were beset with difficulties; in Parliament the Government's opponents were sharpening their attacks. Disraeli was at the mercy of events, an uncomfortable experience for someone who saw himself as the driver rather than the passenger. Harold Macmillan, Prime Minister from 1957 to 1963, would dryly comment in his premiership on the tendency of events to blow a government off course. As a novelist, however, Disraeli could regain control of the narrative. His last novel, *Endymion*, published in 1881, was a best-seller. (See Annabel Jones, 'Fame and Reputation: A Novelist and his Publisher', pp. 21–28.)

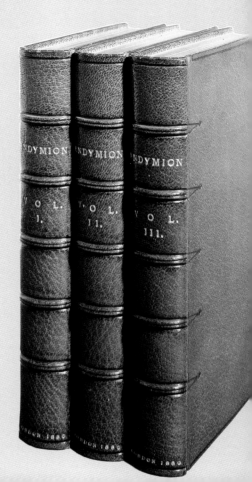

126
Special Editions
12.5 x 10 cm
Disraeli's personal copy of the three-volume
edition of *Endymion*. Like the special editions for
Queen Victoria and Longman they were bound in
green morocco.

Lent by Annabel Jones; reproduced by permission
of Hughenden Manor (The National Trust).

124

Endymion
18.3 x 11.5 cm
Dunston B 735

In his last novel Disraeli returned to the theme of
a young man who arrived 'by his own energies at
the station to which he seemed, as it were born'.
Drawing again on his own life he explored large
themes – political change, the Radical and
Cooperative movements, Free Trade, and
religious issues. He peopled the novel with
figures inspired by his literary and political
contemporaries. The novel, the first by a Prime
Minister, was a huge success. Longman's paid
Disraeli £10,000 for the *Endymion* copyright.

125

Cast of Characters

11 x 7.8 cm
Photostat of Thomas Longman's list from the
Longman archives
University of Reading Longman Archives

Copy of note in pencil by Thomas Norton
Longman (1849–1930) after discussing the real-life
models for the novel's characters with Disraeli's
Private Secretary, Montagu Corry, during his first
visit to Hughenden in August 1880. In his
memoirs, 'Memories personal and various' written
in 1921 (see No. 127), Longman recalled that Corry
had read aloud a good deal of the novel; 'time
passed very pleasantly, and indeed it was not
before two o'clock that we retired' (p. 94).
Longman also noted that Disraeli appeared to
delegate the management of Hughenden to
Corry, who assumed the role of elder son (p. 97).
Longman, the youthful head of the company,
oversaw the publication of the novel.

127

The Gladstone Bag and the manuscript

25.8 x 20.5 cm
Green leather-bound typescript with annotations.
Lent by Annabel Jones

In this extract from his memoirs, 'Memories personal and various', Longman recounts (pp. 99–101) his return visit to Hughenden in September to collect the manuscript of *Endymion*. His awe at the prospect of the meeting was soon mixed with dismay when he realized the bag he'd brought for the purpose was a Gladstone bag – a capacious holdall with two equally-sized compartments, named after the Liberal leader. In the candle-lit gloom Disraeli either didn't notice this or forebore to comment as his manuscript was transferred from his three dispatch boxes. Longman noted Disraeli's 'curious nervous anxiety… to part with so precious and dear a child'. Mr Baum was the butler.

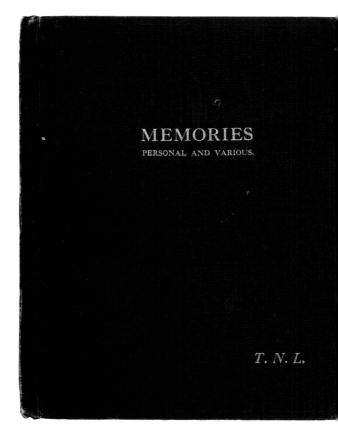

MEMORIES

PERSONAL AND VARIOUS.

T. N. L.

100

saying one word more than was absolutely necessary. The door being opened slowly, solemnly, carefully, mysteriously I followed the ex-premier as he trod lightly along the passage to my apartment Having arrived safely and closing the door with extra precaution he remarked "I am most anxious none of my servants shall know anything about this; that is why I am so careful!"

Our valuable burden having been deposited on the table, Lord Beaconsfield with a sigh of relief remarked "There, but what are you going to do with it?" This was a regular poser as I had not the slightest idea what to do with so precious an article for some fifteen hours or so. A happy thought flashed across my mind - my "Gladstone bag"! I luckily stopped in time, but alas my suggestion only created fresh complications. "Excellent idea" said his Lordship, but my bag was nowhere to be found! It had simply vanished! Awful thought that Mr Baum had done this on purpose! Of course we could not ring to ask Mr Baum what had become of it as that would excite too much suspicion. So hunt for it ourselves we must. We looked under the bed, in the wardrobes, in every corner, but no, nothing could be found.

At last it occurred to me that perhaps it might be in the dressing room just outside, so I went to look, and much to our relief there it was! I immediately carried it off to my room and there under the very eye of the author deposited the three volumes in my little portmanteau. Nothing could have been more comic than the whole proceeding. The curious nervous anxiety

101

so precious and dear a child were so remarkably quaint, and then the author and publisher hunting about all over the place for my Gladstone bag, gave the whole affair so comic a flavour that it was I think quite worthy of a cartoon in Punch. After placing the third volume in its temporary resting place Lord Beaconsfield turned to me and said, "but Mr Longman, how about your wardrobe?" "Oh, there will be plenty of room for that," I replied, but this did not satisfy my host at all and he pressed me to allow him to be of service. "Mr Baum can supply you with any variety of portmanteau if you only ask him", continued Lord Beaconsfield, but I assured him it was quite unnecessary.

Having thus at last accomplished the solemn task of the formal delivery of the MS, we returned to his Lordship's room and in a very few minutes finished my part of the business by paying him a cheque and taking his receipt.

On sitting down for our tête-à-tête dinner, the first thing Lord Beaconsfield said was "Now Mr Longman, we will be like two gentlemen at their Club, pray take your time and do not hurry your dinner. I often wait a quarter of an hour between the courses I knew exactly what he meant - don't you bore me with talking, and I will not bore you. The soup came, the fish came, not a word

128
A fatal chill
17.8 x 11.3 cm
Dep. Hughenden 82/4, fols. 265–6

As the author of a runaway bestseller Disraeli purchased a seven-year lease on 19 Curzon Street, W1, in January 1881. It was the first time he had been able to purchase a house with his own money. Curzon Street was the scene of only one dinner party, on 10 March, to which seventeen guests were invited. Disraeli's health was already failing. The east wind cut into him as he made his way home on 22 March. The chill developed into bronchitis and the spiral of decline began. The house soon witnessed a procession of concerned visitors, including his old political rival Gladstone.

Queen Victoria grew concerned. Before setting off for Osborne on 5 April she wrote this, her last, letter to Disraeli. It was accompanied by primroses from Windsor and the promise to send more primroses from Osborne. Victoria had thought of going to visit him but considered it better to let him rest and looked forward to seeing him when they returned. 'You are ...constantly in my thoughts, & I wish could do anything to cheer you.' Disraeli's reputed final reference to Victoria, when asked if he wanted her to be called to his bedside, was 'No, it is better not. She would only ask me to take a message to Albert.'

Disraeli died in the early hours of 19 April on the anniversary of Byron's death. At his bedside were Corry, who had returned from accompanying his sick sister to Algeria, Sir Philip Rose, Lord Barrington (Lord Derby's former secretary who was standing in for Corry) and his three doctors: Kidd (a homeopath), Bruce and Quain. His last recorded words were, 'I had rather live but I am not afraid to die'. Just before he slipped into unconsciousness he is said to have stirred, moving forward as he did when rising to speak in Parliament.

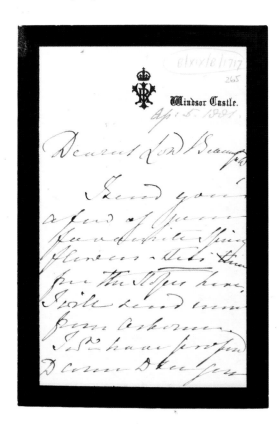

129
Honouring Mary Anne's request
18 x 23 cm
Dep. Hughenden 24/2, fols. 4–5

The original of this letter was written in June 1856 by Mary Anne. Aware that she was likely to die before him she asks Disraeli to leave instructions that they be buried together, 'whatever distance you may die from England'. She wishes God to bless and comfort her 'perfect husband' and, emotionally generous as always, encourages him to remarry or possibly to travel. Corry, now Lord Rowton, had difficulty deciphering her handwriting in 1881. He noted that the original letter had been placed beside Disraeli's heart when he'd been buried in the Hughenden vault the previous

month. Disraeli left instructions that he should be buried simply in the small church at Hughenden, foregoing the honour of a state funeral in Westminster Abbey or St Paul's to which he was entitled.

It fell to Gladstone, as Prime Minister, to offer a state funeral but his response to Disraeli's instructions was ambivalent. While he approved of Disraeli's intention to be buried beside Mary Anne, he was dismissive of what he termed Disraeli's 'playacting' and lack of 'geniuneness'.[24]

130

Disraeli's funeral, 26 April 1881

'Lord Beaconsfield's cortège outside Hughenden
Church' by Alfred Maile 'from a sketch done on
the spot', 1881.
Watercolour, 30.5 x 36.8 cm, reproduced by
permission of Hughenden Manor (The National
Trust).

Among the mourners at the funeral were the
Prince of Wales, three leading Liberals (lords
Rosebery and Hartingdon and Sir William
Harcourt); all bar one of Disraeli's last cabinet;
close friends and family, and young Longman.
A huge crowd gathered as unofficial mourners.
Gladstone's absence was criticized. But when he
came to deliver the formal tribute in the House,
struggling to overcome what Roy Jenkins
describes as his 'incomprehension' of Disraeli, he
alighted on the one aspect of Disraeli he
respected: his political courage – though inwardly
probably dismissing it as that of a gambler.[25]

131

Funeral card

32.3 x 21.5 cm
MS. Harcourt dep. 252, fol. 189

Sir William Harcourt's card for attending
Disraeli's funeral. The corner may probably have
been torn as he was admitted, as there is an
identical tear in that of Thomas Longman's card.

110

wrote to Mr Henry Reeve after the funeral.[x]

    April 28th. - The sad ceremony I had the honour of attending the day before yesterday will for ever live in the memory of all who were present. Nothing would have been more simple in its character, nothing more striking in its solemnity, and nothing in more strict accordance with his wishes. I may well say I shall not forget so great an occasion, not only from the fact that the ceremony was the burial of a great man, but from the very select band of followers I had the privilege of joining. There were only 120 invitations sent out, and all these were not made use of.

    I travelled down in a saloon carriage with Drs Quain, Bruce, Lord Lytton, Lord Alington, Count Munster, with all of whom I had a very pleasant conversation. Sir William Harcourt, Lord Rosebery, the Danish Minister, and another ambassador were also in the carriage; so I had plenty of good company. I had a little conversation with poor Lord Rowton, and thanked him for thinking of me. "Not at all," he said; "I am quite sure it would be his wish that you should be here today." This was, to say the least of it, gratifying.

    The persons who appeared to be most touched were poor Bruce and Lord Henry Lennox. On our return to the Manor about fifty of us went into the drawing-room to hear the will read, and a very interesting document it proved to be. It is perfectly clear Lord Beaconsfield contemplated a good deal of publication. After the reading was finished and those present had mostly left the room, I waited behind a little for the three Princes to move first; and, much to my surprise, the Duke of Connaught turned round, and shook me by the hand. This little incident makes it all a peculiarly interesting and eventful day. We all returned to town together (I mean the Princes and the guests); and I think I may safely say that a train never arrived at Paddington Station with a more distinguished company on board.

    As I walked up from the church I could not help thinking that the last time I walked up the hill I had poor Lord B. on my arm. The demand for "Endymion" is very great, and in fact, the demand for all his novels is greater than we can meet. We are printing night and day to keep the trade supplied.

---

[x] This letter has already appeared in the "Life and Correspondence of Henry Reeve, C.B."

189

HUGHENDEN CHURCH.

Tuesday, April 26th, 1881.

———✠———

Admit *Sir W. Vernon Harcourt MP*

132

'The sad ceremony'

26 x 19 cm

This account of the funeral is taken from Longman's memoir, 'Memories personal and various', p. 110 (see No. 127). Perhaps Disraeli would have been cheered to know that the demand for his novels was so great that Longmans were 'printing night and day to keep the trade supplied'.

134
Primrose League
Enamel and gilt medal made by T. & J. Bragg,
Birmingham
12 x 6 cm
MS. Primrose League adds. 1

The Primrose League, founded in 1883 to recruit
and maintain support for the Conservative Party,
drew on ideas of the medieval past for its
organization. Membership was graded one (the
lowest) to five. Star medals were awarded to
Knights and Dames who had made an outstand-
ing contribution to furthering the principles of
the League. This one includes bars for Queen
Victoria's 1887 Jubilee and the 1898 Sudan
campaign's Battle of Omdurman, in which the
young Winston Churchill fought.

133
Primrose plate
24 cm
Glazed Staffordshire plate, 1886
Lent by a private collector

This octagonal plate has a monochrome image of
Disraeli framed by his favourite flowers,
primroses, and topped by an earl's coronet.
Disraeli was one of several leading political
figures depicted on ceramic wares. Portraits of
several of his contemporaries including Lord
Randolph Churchill, Lord Salisbury, Sir Stafford
Northcote, Joseph Chamberlain, Gladstone, and
the Irish leader Charles Parnell featured in
various series.

THE REFORM BILL RECEIVING THE KING'S ASSENT BY ROYAL COMMISSION;
ANNO DOMINI. JUNE VII. MDCCCXXXII.

135
1832 Reform Bill

Engraving, 75 x 56 cm, of '1832 Reform Bill receiving the King's assent by Royal Commission, June 7, 1832' by William Walker, June 1836. Reproduced by permission of Philip Waller, Merton College, Oxford.

The scene shows the Houses of Parliament before the re-building by Barry and Pugin; the light from the lunette window suggests the dawn of a new era.

THEATRE ROYAL
ST. STEPHEN'S, WESTMINSTER.

Proprietor, - - - - MR. JOHN BULL.

Under the Patronage of Her Majesty the Queen.
FULL STRENGTH OF COMPANY 658.
Re-appearance of old Favourites, and probable last appearance of Messrs Lowe, Bruce and Ayrton, in their Present Characters.
On this and every evening during the week, will be played the Serio-Comic Drama of

BEGGAR
YOUR
NEIGHBOUR
OUT OF DOORS.

Supposed to run for ever, but may be cut short by Accident or Revolution.

THE CHIEF CHARACTERS WILL BE SUSTAINED BY

W. E. Gladstone, a Clever Cabinet Maker, who being a Scotchman is not expected to supply us with anything in the shape of wit.

Ben D'Israeli, a political wandering Jew, who left the *old clothes line* to become a *representative of Bucks*.

Bob Lowe, a naughty boy who played with the matches and burnt his fingers.

Right Hon. E. Horsman, who, as he sat for Cockermouth for 26 years, may be fairly called a Hors(e)man that knows how to keep his seat.

Ayrton the Amiable, a *cold-*hearted cynic, who is never happy except when in *hot* water.

Tom Hughes, whose *Hughes*fulness is variously estimated.

Right Hon. H. B. W. Brand, who is called *the Speaker* because it is his duty to preserve *silence*.

Bernal Osborne, Irish Low Comedian.

Isaac Butt, who, while seeking the *mantle* of O'Connell, will probably end by falling in with the *Pelisse*.

Right Hon. Hugh Culling E. Childers, (descended from the celebrated Flying Childers), a Horse Marine discharged from the Admiralty Board.

W. H. Smith, (a rare name, but by no means a rara avis) who is continually making speeches on the Thames Embankment, which is quite as illegal as though he made them in the park.

C. Seely, the discoverer of Iron Pigs, an entirely new breed of animals, whose flesh is pronounced to be exceedingly solid, but somewhat tougher than, and not so nutritious as Australian beef.

Right Hon. J. Stansfield, a wise man of the yeast.

Sir John Duke Coleridge, a man of few words, born in Devonshire, probably *Torquay*.

Porters by Messrs Bass, Stansfield, Watney, Wethered & Co.

SCENE I.—Woods and Forests—A lot of *Sticks*!
SCENE II.—Board of Trade—A *deal* of Humbug!
Synopsis of Incidents.

OPENING SCENE:—Brown discovered on the Throne—Another Royal Marriage—Great outcry of Pauper Children—Minors who wont work—Cheering prospects for Ratepayers—The enforcement of the law for the Separation of Married Paupers. Division of the Land, a *dirty* transaction, Something brewing, which Bass says is not Burton, though it may be *Bitter*, Apotheosis of the Agricultural Labourer. The Admiralty Board *at sea*—A lot of old women in washing tubs bound for the *Scilly* islands—Education Board, its members seen splitting religious straws, children and parents, in the background, anxiously awaiting the end. Duchy of Cornwall—Great Mining Feat, Prince of Wales, Chief miner, striking a *lode* of *Tin* in the House of Commons, (Supposed value £64,000 per annum).—Colonial Office—Officers all *abroad*—Searching for the Great Globe in Leicester Square, now a *Baron* spot, though a little *Brook* has been found running through it. Exchequer Office—*Lowe* state of the Funds. War Department—Battle of Fox hill, capture of the *Green Prince*. The Woolwich Infant discovered to be ruptured. Application to Coles. The High price of Coles. Department of the Lord Chamberlain, the author presenting his Bills, sudden deaths of the Lord Chamberlain, Vice Chamberlain, Comptroller and Chief Clerk, through excessive laughter, causing a saving to the nation of upwards of £3000 per annum.

FINALE.—The
𝔚hig-𝔗ory 𝔠rew overcome by the 𝔖erfs.

A Triumph of scenic art, drawn by Britannia, who ceased ruling the waves in order that it might be finished in time.

Note—As the Ship goes down, the Duke of Argyle is found at his post.

Conductor ... ... Mr. Speaker.
Scotch Fiddle ... ... Mr. Bruce.
Jew (s) Harper ... ... Mr. Disraeli.
Lyres.—Too numerous to particularise and not altogether safe.
Supplemented by the Pope's Brass Band. (N.B.—Warranted all cracked.)

ADMISSION BY TICKETS ONLY.

136

'Beggar your neighbour'

47 x 19 cm

John Johnson Collection Gladstone folder I (I)

This spoof playbill for the fictional Theatre Royal, St Stephen's, Westminster, advertised the appearance of Disraeli 'a political wandering Jew who left the old clothes line to become a representative of Bucks' and Gladstone a 'Clever Cabinet Minister' but as Scotchman unlikely to be witty. Although both men are lampooned the caricature of Disraeli is the darker.

MR W. E. GLADSTONE

Mʀ W. E. GLADSTONE
THE "GRAND OLD MAN"
HIS BIOGRAPHY IN MICROGRAPHICAL TYPE
THE PICTURE CONTAINS **41,600** LETTERS DISTINCTLY READABLE

137
Disraeli and Gladstone
38 x 51 cm
John Johnson Collection Gladstone folder 1

In this twin portrait in micrographical type 44,200 characters depict Disraeli and 41,600 Gladstone. The words are in English. It was produced by J. Sofer at 50 rue de Rambuteau, Paris.

138
Immortalized in marble
Statue (height 216 cm) of Benjamin Disraeli by C. B. Birch

Disraeli wears the robes of the Chancellor of the Exchequer with which he refused to part, and a fur-trimmed cloak. The statue stands in the loggia at Hughenden.
Reproduced by permission of Hughenden Manor (The National Trust).

LORD BEACONSFIELD

HIS BIOGRAPHY IN MICROGRAPHICAL TYPE

THE PICTURE CONTAINS **44,200** LETTERS DISTINCTLY READABLE

139

A Prime-Ministerial salute

29.5 x 21 cm

MS. Wilson c. 1699

In 1977, the year after his surprise retirement, the
former Labour Prime Minister Harold (later
Lord) Wilson (1916-95) made a television series,
A Prime Minister on Prime Ministers. During the
filming at Hughenden he was photographed
standing next to this statue of Disraeli.[26] In his
draft commentary Wilson assesses the contribution of 'probably the most fascinating and
inscrutable Prime Minister Britain had ever had'.

XXXX ****** XXXX

[And now —] Disraeli.

Probably the most fascinating and inscrutable Prime Minister Britain has ever had for more than 30 years in Politics and as a man ... in his youth, universally regarded as a charlatan, poseur, social climber, outsider crashing to get in. A community speculator before he was 21, & a buried periodical publisher soon afterwards — saddling himself with massive debts almost for life.

Determined to enter Politics, without any principles or party beliefs. Flirting with the Radicals, then the Tories; at as radical candidate accepting £500 for his expenses from the Tories — a grant procured by a Tory Lord Chancellor, Lyndhurst with whom he shared a mistress.

Elected as a Tory soon afterwards destroying his leader, Peal for the repeal of the Corn Laws, ... the most devastating invective ever seen in Politics — less than 3 years later, throwing over protectionism as "not only dead, but damned."

Years of sitting in opposition with the rump of the Tories — and two minority governments — in the first, as Chancellor of the Exchequer, getting his budget wrong & nursing up his tax schedules. In the second, as Prime Minister, beating the Tories in the race to carry a long overdue Reform Bill, not caring what the Bill contained, switching & switching until he caught Gladstone & the Liberals on the wrong foot, & winning through. Six more years in opposition — then a victory, a secure majority for at least six years ahead.

Disraeli was emancipated. ... he carried through the social reforms he wanted ... Still more he moved to a new vision of Britain's role in the world, such as few have dared to seek. Powerful again in Europe — breaking up the alliances which stood in the way;

When the Turkish Empire was in its agonies, declining rotting, he stood by to prevent a Russian take-over in an Eastern Mediterranean, which he feared would threaten the Canal & the route to India.

369

—2—

His diplomatic triumph at the Congress of Berlin, and the cheers in the streets when he returned bringing "Peace with Honour", as he claimed, was at one with the new vision of Empire, and the new dignity of the Queen-Empress.

A break-through for Disraeli, & in a real sense, a break-through for Britain — at the peak of her power, her diplomacy, as her navy — with the new ironclads — at the peak of their force.

... The reason why he stands so high among Britain's Prime Ministers, regardless of party, is that he had the personal vision, and the skill to create a vision for his country, his Queen, and his people.

——

1/4

Notes

1   The Sephardi, one of the two main groups of Jews, the other being the Ashkenazi; each with a distinctive liturgy. 'Di' means 'son of'. Robert Blake, *Disraeli* (London, 1966), pp. 3–4, 6.

2   John Murray Archive, Box 13.

3   For a discussion of Disraeli as a young novelist see Jane Ridley, *The Young Disraeli* (London, 1995).

4   Charles Richmond's essay, 'Disraeli's Education' in Richmond and Paul Smith (eds.), *The Self-Fashioning of Disraeli, 1818–51* (Cambridge, 1998), pp. 34, 182, n. 80.

5   Sarah Bradford, *Disraeli* (New York, 1983), p. 90.

6   Blake, *Disraeli*, p. 150.

7   Of the five volumes of Smythe correspondence mentioned by Disraeli in 1873 (Blake, *Disraeli*, p. 170) only five letters now survive. Smythe fought Col. Romilly – fellow MP for Canterbury – in the last duel in England in 1852.

8   Disraeli's Preface to the 1870 edition of the novels, quoted in Blake, *Disraeli*, p. 193.

9   MS. Wilberforce c. 13, fols. 207–8, 30 November 1862.

10 Dep. Hughenden 307/1, fols. 1–2, printed, letter 1484, M. G. Wiebe, Mary S. Millar, Ann P. Robson (eds.), *Benjamin Disraeli Letters Volume VI: 1852–1856* (Toronto, 1997), p. 226: Disraeli to Philip Rose.

11 *Disraeli Letters VI*, p. xiii.

12 Blake, *Disraeli*, p. 313.

13 Roy Jenkins, *Gladstone* (London, 1995), p. 268. Jenkins quoting Blake quoting Beaverbrook on Lloyd George.

14 Ibid., p. 270.

15 Dep. Hughenden 110/2, fols. 216–9, 22 December 1866.

16 Jenkins, *Gladstone*, p. 270.

17 Blake, *Disraeli*, p. 518; Bradford, *Disraeli*, p. 289.

18 Bradford, *Disraeli*, p. 295.

19 Kenneth Morgan, *Callaghan: A Life* (Oxford, 1997), p. 476. Callaghan's Cabinet style was the most managerial since Attlee.

20 Paul Smith, *Disraeli: A Brief Life* (New York, 1996; reissued Cambridge, 1999), p. 77.

21 A. N. Wilson, *The Victorians* (London, 2002), p. 388.

23 Jenkins, *Gladstone*, p. 405.

24 Andrew Roberts, *Salisbury: Victorian Titan* (London, 1999), p. 254. Salisbury, writing to Lord John Manners, was already in mourning for his sister.

25 Jenkins, *Gladstone*, p. 459.

26 Ibid., p. 459.

27 Philip Ziegler, *Wilson: The Authorised Life of Lord Wilson of Rievaulx* (London, 1993). Illustration No. 23, between pp. 466–7.

Further Reading

Robert Blake, *The Conservative Party from Peel to Churchill* (London, 1970).

Robert Blake, *Disraeli* (London, 1966).

Sarah Bradford, *Disraeli* (N.Y., 1983).

[The Disraeli Project] J. A. W. Gunn, M.G. Wiebe, J. B. Conacher, John Matthews, Mary S. Millar, *et. al.* (eds), *Benjamin Disraeli Letters I– (1815–)*, (6 vols. to date) (Toronto and London, 1982–).

Maurice Edelman, *Disraeli in Love* (London, 1972).

Todd M. Endelman and Tony Kushner (eds.), *Disraeli's Jewishness* (London, 2002).

Michael and Mollie Hardwick, *Writers' Houses A Literary Journey in England* (London, 1968).

Angus Hawkins, *British Party Politics, 1852-1886* (Basingstoke, 1998).

Roy Jenkins, *Gladstone* (London, 1995; rpt. 1996).

Margaret O. Macmillan, *Peacemakers: the Paris Conference of 1919 and its Attempt to End War* (London, 2001).

W. F. Monypenny and G. E. Buckle, *The Life of Benjamin Disraeli, Earl of Beaconsfield*, 6 vols. (London, 1910-20).

Timothy Mowl, *William Beckford* (London, 1998).

Hughenden Manor, Buckinghamshire: A Property of the National Trust (London [Country Life for the National Trust], 1997).

Hesketh Pearson, *Dizzy: The Life and Nature of Benjamin Disraeli, Earl of Beaconsfield* (London, 1951; rpt. 2001).

John Plunkett, *Queen Victoria: First Media Monarch* (Oxford, 2003).

Charles Richmond & Paul Smith, *The Self-Fashioning of Disraeli, 1818-1851* (Cambridge, 1998).

Jane Ridley, *The Young Disraeli* (London, 1995).

Andrew Roberts, *Salisbury: Victorian Titan* (London, 1999).

Paul Smith, *Disraeli, A Brief Life* (New York, 1996; Cambridge, 1999).

John Vincent, *Disraeli, Derby and the Conservative Party: Journals and Memoirs of Edward Henry, Lord Stanley 1849-1869* (Hassocks, 1978).

John Vincent (ed.), *A selection from the diaries of Edward Henry Stanley, 15th Earl of Derby (1826-93): Between September 1869 and March 1878* (London, 1994).

John Vincent (ed.), *The Diaries of Edward Henry Stanley, 15th Earl of Derby (1826-93) Between 1878 and 1893: A Selection* (Oxford, 2003).

A.N. Wilson, *The Victorians* (London, 2002).

Electronic resources include:

The National Trust <www.thenationaltrust.org.uk>.

The National Register of Archives <www.hmc.gov.uk> for listing of nationwide holdings of Disraeli correspondence the bulk of which are in the British Library <www.bl.uk>.

The Disraeli Project <http://qsilver.queensu.ca/english/dismen.html>.

<knebworthhouse.com/history/history.html> for information on the 1st Earl of Lytton.

The Rothschild Research Forum <www.rothschildarchive.org>; <www.waddesdon.org.uk>.